The Case for Rand Paul

I0424027

Essays in Defense of the Presidential Candidacy

of Senator Rand Paul

By Lee Enochs

Introduction

Throughout the annals of American history there have been bold patriot-citizens who have stood up against the tyranny and repression against seemingly insurmountable odds.

One such individual is Rand Paul. On April 2, 2014 the Junior Senator from Kentucky announced that he is running for the 2016 Republican Nomination for President of the United States and millions of Americans around the country are overjoyed that out of the multiplicity and smorgasbord of Republican candidates currently running the GOP nomination, there is at least one viable candidate that truly cares about the rapid erosion and evisceration of our civil liberties.

Many Republicans across the United States have become increasingly dissatisfied with politics as usual in Washington D.C. and want the elected officials we have sent there to actually do the things that promised during their respective campaigns.

It seems as though there is currently an observable and disheartening pattern occurring in American politics wherein after a person is elected to Congress, he or she forgets their constituencies and the promises and policies their respective campaigns were predicated on.

Additionally, there are many rank and file Republicans who have become discontented with the current state of the

Grand Old Party. Too often, campaign rhetoric notwithstanding, there is very little substantial difference between the Republicans and Democrats on spending and other important economic issues.

While many Republicans talk a big game about reigning in the national debt that is now over $18 trillion dollars, they still perpetuate the massive deficit spending and pork subsidies that dominate politics as usual in America.

Another serious issue facing Republicans across this country pertains to our civil liberties and personal privacy. The evidence demonstrates that under the guise of the Patriot Act, the Federal government is spying on its own citizenry and readily has access to our most private personal information.

The fact is that American government is involved in the bulk collection of our private and personal data from every American with a cell phone. We have an urgent need in this country to end the NSA's illegal bulk data collection and domestic spying programs as outlined in the 4th Amendment.

We need national leaders in Washington D.C. that will safeguard and protect our constitutionally guaranteed civil liberties and right to privacy. As Senator Rand Paul says, "the phone records of law-abiding citizens are none of the government's damn business!"

Because America needs a proven leader who sincerely cares about our civil liberties, halting Washington's runaway spending and eradicating the national debt, I have come to the conclusion that Senator Rand Paul is the most viable candidate for the US Presidency.

For this reason I have chosen to vote for Rand Paul in the coming 2016 Republican primaries. As a life-long member of the GOP, I have grown weary of RINO (Republican in name only) members of the Republican Party and want truly conservative candidates to represent us. For this reason and many, many more, I have chosen to write this book and to encourage my family and friends to vote for Rand Paul for President in 2016.

I want to be clear from the onset that I do not speak in any official capacity for the Rand Paul campaign. I did not contact the Rand Paul campaign and neither did the Rand Paul campaign contact me. There are far more qualified and experienced writers out there who can do Rand Paul a lot better service in writing a defense of his Presidential aspirations.

 I take all the blame for any mistakes this book makes. However, I have written this book out of love for my country and the party of my youth. I am just a life-long Republican who has made up his mind about who he wants to be President in 2016. All my life I have been looking for a true fiscal conservative to become President and I believe Rand Paul is the best candidate to fill our nation's highest office.

America is on the brink of certain systemic and economic catastrophe and the powers that be in Washington do not care to change this crisis of cataclysmic proportions. As I write this, America faces am almost insurmountable and most certainly unsustainable $18 trillion dollar debt.

I am also voting for Rand Paul for President because he is advocating a Balanced Budget Amendment to deal with the catastrophic economic crisis that is currently plaguing America. Another determining factor in my support for Rand Paul for President in 2016 pertains to the rule of law in this country.

Over the last year, many of our major cities have plummeted into abject crime and violence. I am convinced that Rand Paul will attempt to rid our major cities of the violent crime that threatens to destroy them. I am also voting for Rand Paul because he is currently advocating the complete defunding of Planned Parenthood and rejects abortion on demand.

As a devout Evangelical Christian, I personally belief that all life matters and that every human being has been created in the image of God and is endowed by their creator with the unalienable rights to life, liberty and the pursuit of happiness.

Since the 1973 *Roe vs. Wade* Supreme Court verdict to legalize abortion on demand, the lives of close to 60 million children have been lost due to abortion. I am convinced that Rand Paul is believes in the right to life and wants to defund Planned Parenthood.

I am convinced that Rand Paul stands for the rights of the unborn. I am also convinced that Rand Paul believes in the principles of individualism and individual rights.

That is, I believe the Junior Senator from the fine state of Kentucky believes that each person has the right to be secure in their life, liberty and property. I believe that Rand Paul believes that these rights are not given to us by the federal government or by collective society. Rand Paul believes that these rights were given to us by God and are inherent in the nature of human beings.

I believe that Rand Paul is a sincere proponent and operates by the axiom that the best government is the least amount of government. That is, I am voting for Rand Paul because he believes that government has grown far too big and intrusive in our personal lives. For these reasons and more I am proud to make the case for Senator Rand Paul.

The following book is a collection of essays in defense of the presidential candidacy of Senator Rand Paul. I wrote these essays over a period of six months as I reflected upon each of the candidates running for the Republican nomination. This book contains the reasons why I believe Rand Paul is the best candidate for President of any party. I believe Rand Paul alone has the wisdom and vision to carry this country into the third decade of the new millennium.

As a Republican with distinctly Libertarian views on economics and the relationship between American citizens and their government, I believe that this country needs bold and innovative leaders who will work together to reduce the staggering national debt and size of government. I believe Rand Paul is that man and that Rand Paul alone has the courage of conviction to balance the federal budget.

Rand Paul believes that individual liberty is a precious commodity and that this liberty is worth fighting for. Rand Paul believes that every American has certain unalienable and natural rights such as the right to life, liberty and the pursuit of happiness. Rand Paul also believes in the importance of the free enterprise system, private property. Senator Paul also believes it is also of paramount importance to preserve our individual liberties from the encroaching power of the State.

This book gives a comprehensive and compelling argument for why I believe Rand Paul should be our next President.

A collection of essays I have written since Rand Paul first announced he is running for the Republican nomination, "The Case for Rand Paul" is written from the heart. I pull no punches on why I believe Rand Paul is the best choice to lead America as our next President.

I have a confession to make, I am a book worm. I am an ideas guy. That is, I have spent my entire life reading the classic works of Western Civilization trying to make sense of this thing called life.

While I spend the vast majority of my days studying Christian theology, over the last decade or so, my thoughts have turned to politics (from Greek: πολιτικός politikos, definition "of, for, or relating to citizens") is the practice and theory of influencing other people.

While politics gets a bad rap in America today, the fact is, none of us can escape the reality that politics plays an essential part of each our daily lives.

From the taxes we pay to the speed limits on our city streets, essentially everything we do is interconnected to the political process and politicians at the local, state-wide and national level.

We can all acknowledge that there is something fundamentally wrong with the political system in America. Truth be told, it is broken and near irrevocable collapse.

Unwise and unthrifty politicians have gambled and lost with their spending frenzy. Unbridled spending on wars, entitlements and social welfare programs has brought America near economic catastrophe.

Our national debt is now close to $19 trillion dollars and accumulates each and every day. We are now spending approximately $7 million dollars per minute as a nation and this mad spending frenzy is clearly unsustainable.

Of all the current Republican candidates now vying for the GOP's Presidential nomination, only Rand Paul has a viable plan to balance our federal budget and only spend what comes in. Only Rand Paul has the courage to work to eradicating our national debt.

Similarly, Rand Paul wants to audit the fed and repeal the entire IRS tax code-more than 70,000 pages of it, with a low, broad-based tax of 14.5% on individuals and businesses.

Furthermore, Senator Rand Paul has promised to repeal Obamacare and federal funding for Planned Parenthood.

Rand Paul is also the only Republican Presidential candidate that has a comprehensive plan to guarantee the maximization of our civil liberties. Senator Paul wants to end the NSA's bulk collection of our personal data from our cell phones and wants to guarantee our right to privacy as afforded to us by the U.S. Constitution.

Rand Paul is on a crusade to end politics as usual in Washington D.C. He also wants to balance the federal budget, eradicate our national debt and ensure our civil liberties. For these reasons and many more I have joined the Rand Paul Revolution. I would like to encourage you to do the same.

Paul strongly advocates the due process of law, freedom of speech, freedom of association, government by consent and the full equality of every American under the law. For these reasons and much more I now present to you "The Case for Rand Paul."

Rand Paul Can Beat the Washington Machine

Is there a conspiracy against Rand Paul, the junior senator of Kentucky and current Republican Presidential candidate? From my vantage point, the answer to this query depends entirely upon what one means by the word *conspiracy*.

Do I believe there is a secret plot and highly coordinated effort by the national news media and the Republican establishment to discredit Rand Paul and thwart his Presidential ambitions? While I find most "conspiracy theories" utterly preposterous and untenable, I do believe there is an interconnectivity of resistance on the part of many of members of the political establishment and news media to give Senator Paul a fair hearing.

This is not to say, that I believe there is a secret "power behind the throne" that is dictating whether or not Rand

Paul can be a viable candidate for the Republican nomination. Yet, I do believe there is something akin to a coordinated effort to defame and discredit Senator Paul in the minds and hearts of the Republican faithful.

I personally believe that many establishment Republicans do not care for Rand Paul's brand of Libertarian conservatism and will do everything in their power to malign and distort Paul's beliefs and policies.

This distortion of Rand Paul's ideas, policy positions and record is then picked up and repeated by conservative magazines and news outlets like National Review and Fox News. This distortion of Paul becomes reality in the minds of voters who have no time to filter such perversions of Rand Paul's views and record.

Anyone that knows anything about the editors of National Review can readily testify that its editors loathe Rand Paul, Libertarianism and Rand's father, Ron.

Much of the open hatred and detestation of Rand Paul comes from hawkish national security conservatives who closely identify with the military industrial complex. Besides the sheer loss of money to agencies and companies that get rich off its connection to the U.S. military, many hawks believe that Rand Paul will be soft on the war on terror and hence jeopardize America's security and standing in the world.

While nothing in Paul's record and policies suggest such a mischaracterization, again, perception is reality for many national security proponents who sense, perhaps correctly, that a President Rand Paul would severely curtail the misappropriation of spending and funds on things we exactly do not need.

To answer the question of whether or not I believe there is a "conspiracy" against Rand Paul by the media and establishment Republicans, yes, in some sense I do believe there is a coordinated resistance to Paul for the reasons I have elucidated above.

For Rand Paul to win the Republican nomination, he will have to fight up hill and think and act outside the box to gain attention to his campaign. Recently a petition has been going around that encourages Rand Paul to do a town hall type debate forum with Bernie Sanders. Such an event may be of a great benefit to Paul who seeks to break out of the box the Republican establishment and news media has tried to contain him in.

A Friend Has Had His "Come to the Donald" Moment

Despite a recent dip in the polls, Donald J. Trump still leads the pack for the Republican nomination by a large margin. During a recent trip to Dallas that happened to coincide with a major Trump event at a prominent sports arena, I saw first-hand the considerable sway that the Donald has over a significant segment of potential Republican primary voters.

Donald Trump has achieved rock star status in the minds and hearts of millions of Republicans and conservative Americans, and I wanted to know why.

My best friend's recent announcement that he is now voting for Donald Trump has also piqued my interest in the Trump phenomena. Is it a flash in the pan, here today, but gone tomorrow?

Or is Donald Trump mania a real thing that we long-time Republicans will have to deal with for the foreseeable future? Could the star of the "Celebrity Apprentice" actually win the Republican nomination for President in 2016 and be our nominee next fall?

Intrigued as to why so many conservatives and Republicans are hopping so brazenly on the Donald's bandwagon, especially since Trump was a pro-choice, gun control Democrat very recently, I asked a diehard Trump supporter why he has had a "come to the Donald" moment and is pledging his heart and soul to the billionaire media and real estate mogul.

"The Donald will get things done in Washington," my friend replied, obviously startled that I would dare to question him on why has come out for Donald Trump. "I am tired of a do nothing congress that just sits on their behinds and does nothing," my friend went on to say. "Mr. Trump has proved that he is a man of action," my zealous Trump supporting friend said.

"But, wasn't Trump a liberal Democrat only a few years ago who recently supported Obamacare, partial birth abortion, gun control and high taxes?" I asked sincerely.

"That was three long years ago, besides people change. Didn't Ronald Reagan himself switch from being a New

Deal Democrat to being a conservative Republican?" my friend replied.

When I asked what policies of Trump my friend supported, he responded that Donald Trump is a man of deeds and not words. Furthermore he said that he had a "gut feeling" deep down inside his belly that Donald would bring change and make America great again.

"But, isn't that exactly what Obama and his supporters said, just seven years ago?" I retorted, wondering how an educated man like my friend could place his hope and trust in a political candidate with a proven track record of supporting liberal policies without a shred of objective evidence.

"The Donald is different," my friend said finally, believing deep within that Donald J. Trump is the man for this hour. "When Donald Trump is elected President, he will throw those bums out of Washington, build a massive fence around America that will keep all the bad guys and illegal immigrants out," my friend stated. Just exactly how was never exactly answered by my friend who received Donald Trump into his life.

On Ben Carson and the Constitutionality of a Muslim President

All hell seems to have broken out in the Republican Party. Or, in the case of Neurosurgeon turned novice Presidential candidate Ben Carson, all heaven has busted loose.

Specifically, I am referring to Dr. Carson's imprudent and greatly unconstitutional statement that he would not support a Muslim being President of the United States of America. Dr. Carson said, and I quote in verbatim on NBC's "Meet the Press,"

"I would not advocate that we put a Muslim in charge of this nation. I absolutely would not agree with that,"

Dr. Carson's shocking statement comes after GOP front-runner Donald Trump taking a question from a campaign rally attendee who said, "We have a problem in this country; it's called Muslims."

Such comments, while popular in certain segments in American conservatism, are most certainly contrary to the express intention and statement of the First Amendment that specifically safeguards the freedom of religion in this country.

While I, myself am a devout Christian, I cannot concur with Dr. Carson's sentiments and question if the good Doctor has the Constitutional knowledge and where all to be a good Commander and Chief.

While I might contest on doctrinal grounds various tenets of Islam, the U.S. Constitution does not give a religious litmus test and qualification for those seeking the Presidency.

The U.S Constitution is very clear as to Presidential eligibility.

ARTICLE II, SECTION 1, CLAUSE 5 says:

No Person except a natural born Citizen, or a Citizen of the United States, at the time of the Adoption of this Constitution, shall be eligible to the Office of President; neither shall any Person be eligible to that Office who shall not have attained to the Age of thirty five Years, and been fourteen Years a Resident within the United States.

The First Amendment of the Bill of Rights, a foundational legal document of our country states;

"Congress shall make no law respecting an establishment of religion."

While I understand why Carson and others feel the way they do about Muslims and other non-Christian religions in America, the fact is, what Carson has said about not wanting a Muslim to be President, has no legal precedent. I also know that Carson and other conservatives are Evangelical in their religious orientation and so I am. However, there have been many Presidents and Presidential candidates that have not been Evangelical Christian.

Case in point, Thomas Jefferson, at best was a deist who published a Bible deemed heretical by many Christians at the time, for omitting references to supernatural phenomenon. William Howard Taft was President from 1909 to 1913 was a Unitarian whose church denied the orthodox Christian view of the Trinity and the Deity of

Christ. Taft later served as the Chief Justice to the U.S. Supreme Court until his death in 1930.

Furthermore, John F. Kennedy was Roman Catholic and former Massachusetts Governor and 2012 Republican nominee Mitt Romney was a Mormon. The religious beliefs of these two leaders of their respective parties did not disqualify or preclude them from running for President.

I am left wondering if Dr. Ben Carson and others who deny that Muslims should be able to be President have actually read the clauses in the Constitution that clearly states that Congress shall make no law respecting an establishment of religion and that one's religious beliefs should not factor into whether or not one should be President.

I am not in any way supporting Islam or any other religion in this treatise I am merely suggesting that Carson's comments are not in keeping with the Constitutional idea of the separation of church and state and religious freedom.

If a Muslim cannot be President, who can be? Only Evangelical Christians? Was Mitt Romney not a legitimate candidate because he was a Mormon? Who then decides if a person is "Christian" enough to be President?

Are Ben Carson and his followers not prescribing a religious litmus test to see who can be President and desire to amend the U.S. Constitution where Muslims and all non-Christians need not aspire to the highest office of our land?

Why Debates Matter

We live in an age of American history where mindless reality TV shows and anti-intellectualism prevails and things like cognitive ideas and debates are frowned upon by a large portion of Americans. As a person who has been a chairman of a debating society, I have participated in many formal debates and have given the concept of debate a lot of thought over the years. Contrary to popular opinion debates matter and are ultimately part of our daily lives if we like them or not.

The Merriam / Webster Dictionary defines "debate" as; (a) A contention by words or arguments. (b) The formal discussion of a motion before a deliberative body according to the rules of parliamentary procedure, and (c) A regulated discussion of a proposition between matched sides.

Despite their alleged unpopularity, debates and debating are part of our daily lives whether we know this or not. Many of argue with our friends on why we like one sports team or athlete over another. Others of us debate whether or not a particular movie star hunk or beauty queen is more attractive over another and so on.

While politics and politicians are extremely unpopular in this country right now, deep down inside we know that politics affects us all. From the amount of taxes that are taken out of checks each pay period to how fast we can drive our cars without receiving a ticket, we know very well that politics and government have a direct relationship with our daily lives.

Most of us want American society to work better. Most of us want lower taxes and more freedom to live our lives that way we feel is best. Despite the broken state of the political system in America today, most of us want our politicians to act wisely on our behalf and pass laws that will directly benefit our daily lives and insure a better hope for future generations.

Like it or not, formal and informal debates and debating is part of the political process in America. From our favorite talk show host who debates whether or not President Obama is doing his job well or not to our congressmen and women debating the specifics of a particular piece of legislation, debates directly affect us on a daily basis.

This is why 25 million people tuned into the Fox News Republican Primary debate in August and over 23 million people watched the Republicans debate live on cable television again last week. While it is hard to believe this now, but over 50 million people watched the first televised debate between Barack Obama and Mitt Romney in 2012. Deep down inside we know that debates matter and we want the politicians running for President to be good at debating or suffer the consequence of losing our support.

Debates can make or break a Presidential candidate. Case in point, despite his enormous success as the three term governor of Texas, Rick Perry's dismal performance in a Presidential debate during the 2012 Republican Primary season, destroyed his prospects then and was a major factor in why he recently was the first Republican candidate to bow out of the race this time around. Rick Perry's collapse as a Presidential candidate initially occurred in a Presidential debate and he was never able to overcome a perception that he was a bad debater.

On the other hand, Carly Fiorina's recent smashing success in the first two Republican Primary debates has catapulted her to second in the national polls. Donald Trump's personal attacks against Rand Paul in the CNN Debate made him look cheap and petty. Debates matter my friends, whether or not we like that or not and your favorite Presidential candidate can become a true contender or an afterthought based on his or her debate performance.

A good debate can cause a candidate like Rand Paul, Ted Cruz or Marco Rubio to be the next front runner.

On the Progressive Thought Police

As a person who has lived and studied in some of the most prominent liberal college towns in America, I have heard a lot about tolerance, or being "tolerant," the alleged willingness to tolerate or permit something or an opinion that one does not necessarily agree with.

I have seen up close and very personal, that such claims to tolerance from the left are merely an illusion.

The truth is my friend, liberals and progressive people like Bernie Sanders and Hillary Clinton won't just let you be. That is, they feel especially inclined to inform you whether you like it or not, that they know what is best for your own personal life.

While many liberals and progressives are also irreligious, they are resolute in their confidence that know better than everyone else and are bent on implementing a secularist utopia on this fallen earth. Inherent within this secularist Shangri-La is its own set of intrinsic values and presuppositions.

It is of paramount importance to understand that the left has its own ideas on how this world should operate and if you happen to be of a more conservative or libertarian persuasion, you are an insurrectionist and obstructionist in their enlightened rose garden.

The crux of the issue is that many people on the left will not settle until there is absolute conformity to their pluralistic and politically correct vision of America. While they preach tolerance, they are especially intolerant of those who dare to defy them.

If you want to test someone from the left's alleged "tolerance," try defending Biblical Christianity, traditional marriage, capitalism or the current state of Israel. You will find out quickly how your views are not tolerated by the secular and liberal "elite." The only "heresy" to the progressive left, is conservative orthodoxy.

While there are multifarious ways the left seeks to implement social control, make no mistake it about it my friend, the left thinks it knows better than you on what you should do with your own life and money. It has an elitist mentality and thinks they are simply better than you are at managing your own life, time and monetary resources.

Like Marx, Stalin, Che Guevara, Fidel Castro and other totalitarians before them, many on the progressive left will not allow you to be you. They think they know what is best for you and everyone else. Autonomy and individualism is not allowed. It seems like a tendency of human beings to seek to subjugate one another irrespective of one's political persuasion. Liberty and freedom are not high priorities to those who seek to micromanage everything and everyone. Those who seek to be gods allow no other idols.

The Good, the Bad and the Ugly about Donald Trump

I have lived in Texas and I like the Wild, Wild West. I am also not going to lie to you guys. I love the "Spaghetti Western" films starring Clint Eastwood. In particular, I love the "Good, the Bad and the Ugly," a 1966 Italian epic Spaghetti Western film directed by Sergio Leone, starring Clint Eastwood, Lee Van Cleef, and Eli Wallach in the titular roles of a film some have called the greatest epic ever. I particularly love the iconic music score of this movie.

Now, in the same way "The Good, the Bad and the Ugly" had its good characters and its very bad characters, each of us have good and bad characteristics. Unfortunately some of us have more radical bipolarity than others.

In the circus that is America's political scene, it is doubtful that anyone has as many good, bad and ugly characteristics as Donald Trump.

The Good

As a Rand Paul supporter that takes great umbrage to Donald Trump's personal attacks on my candidate, it is very difficult for me to praise the Donald for anything. Yet, despite my personal reluctance to sing Trump's praises and paint his picture on the Sistine Chapel, there are many good things about the "Celebrity Apprentice."

As an avowed capitalist who has written a book in defense of the free enterprise system, I am very much in support of making money the old fashioned way. Like the old "Smith and Barney" commercials, I believe we have to earn it. While some of Trump's business and real estate transactions might be questionable like allowing some of his enterprises go bankrupt, I believe that Trump has substantially earned his billions of dollars in the right and lawful way.

I also like the fact that has been a successful entertainer with his TV shows. I am not a socialist like Bernie Sanders and do not want to separate Mr. Trump from his substantial wealth. In fact, I would like a little bit of it myself. I personally praise Donald Trump for encouraging Americans to go out and become successful themselves.

The Bad

Yet, despite these good qualities there is a whole lot of bad about Donald J. Trump that his legions of supporters are looking past. These very bad character flaws and outright abusive tendencies will most certainly be seized upon by the national media should Mr. Trump win the Republican nomination next year and face the Democratic candidate.

In the last few months, Donald Trump has managed to recklessly attack and insult Hispanics, women and anyone that dares to disagree with him or oppose his candidacy. Case in point, his crude comments about Carly Fiorina and Rand Paul's looks, conclusively demonstrate, as Rand Paul has pointed out, that Trump lacks the self-control and temperament to be President of the United States of America. Our country's good will and moral standing in the world has suffered enough under Barack Obama, it most certainly will be shipwrecked, if Donald Trump is elected President in November, 2016.

The Ugly

While I do not want to lapse into the same sort of mud-slinging that Donald Trump engages in on an almost daily basis, I will let the reader do his or her own research on the moral life of Donald Trump, who is on record boasting about his myriad of sexual escapades.

His divorces and current marital situation would have caused many an American to take pause in election cycles past. However, we live a brave new world and new millennium where a major Presidential candidate like Trump can be married to a woman who has posed in compromising magazine shoots and it is not considered an issue at all.

My biggest problem about Trump is that he has very little ability not to attack others and make wild and inflammatory accusations and defamations. All these things will most certainly be capitalized on by his Democratic opponents, if he wins the nomination.

As a life-long Republican who has voted in every Presidential election since the 1980's, I might have to sit this one out if Donald J. Trump happens to be my party's nominee.

Why Evangelicals Should Vote for Rand Paul

I am an Evangelical Christian and have studied theology over the course of most of my life. I am a Christ Follower who very much wants to help men and women know Christ and are sons and daughters in the Kingdom of God.

Jesus died on the cross for our sins and rose again from the dead to make citizenship in His kingdom available to all those who would repent of their sins and believe in His name. The earth upon which we now dwell is a very transient and temporal locale. Soon Christ will return from the heavens and make all things new.

Yet, while we have time left, we are commanded by the Word of Christ to be good citizens on this earthy sphere. We are told by the Apostle Peter to "fear God and honor the king" (1 Peter 2:17).

Similarly, we are told by the noble apostle Paul to obey the governing authorities that God has set over us for these political authorities have been ordained by God (Romans 13:1). It is God who raises up rulers and brings them down and all the nations of the world are a drop in a bucket to Almighty God (Isaiah 40:15 and Daniel 2:21).

That is, it is God Himself according to inspired and inerrant Scripture, that decides who shall lead a specific nation of people. It is also God who chooses the means by which a ruler is brought into power or removed from office. Through God's inscrutable wisdom and the mystery of divine providence, He has sovereignly ordained the participatory and Constitutional Democracy that now governs the United States of America.

We the people of these United States believe in the equality of every man, woman and child and believe in the consent of the governed. The Constitution of the United States and the Declaration of Independence states explicitly that each qualified citizen of this nation can be participate in our democratic process and that the consent of the governed is a condition urged by these solemn documents as a requirement of legitimate government.

It states specifically that the authority of our government should depend entirely upon the consent of the people by votes via free elections. Yet our democracy is currently under siege. Forces from within and from without our beloved nation threatens to destroy us as a people and is attempting to subjugate us under the tyranny of a self-professed "elite" few. Many pundits and astute observers of American history are proclaiming the coming 2016 election cycle as the most important time period in our storied history.

In 2016 we will decide if we will continue down the pathway of Obama and the liberal elite's government intervention or if we will change course and be the shining city on a hill envisioned by our forefathers. The time has come for all of us who love America and civil liberties to unite under the banner of freedom that this government of the people, for the people and by the people should not perish from the earth.

Brothers, Sisters and my fellow Countrymen, lend me your ears!

I apologize for my boldness, but I must suggest to you that Senator Rand Paul is the right choice for President in 2016. Before you vote in the coming Republican primaries, I would urge you to take another look at the policies and candidacy of Rand Paul who is standing for our freedom and civil liberties like no other candidate.

I have been a Republican all my life and I believe Rand Paul is the best candidate for this time. Please log on to https://www.randpaul.com/ and get to know Senator Paul.

America is too great to throw it all away on untested and unproven candidates that have never won an election. I urge you to reconsider voting for Rand Paul. Sincerely with Kind Regards, Lee Enochs Princeton, New Jersey

Lee Enochs, (B.A., Southwestern Baptist Theological Seminary), is a graduate student in Princeton, New Jersey and is the President of the Princeton Conservative Club. Lee is also the author of "A Biblical Defense of Capitalism" and the soon to be released new book, "The Case for Rand Paul."

Why Sanders Appearance at Liberty University Was Good for America

 "The Best Government is the Least Amount of Government"

"But examine everything carefully, hold fast to the truth" (1 Thessalonians 5:21).

Earlier this week one of the most important events in recent American history took place. No, I am not referring to the CNN debate as entertaining as that was. In actuality, I am referring to Vermont Senator and current presidential candidate Bernie Sanders appearance at Liberty University.

It was important for all the right reasons since Sanders and the fundamentalist Christian Liberty University are on the absolute polar opposites of the ideological, political, and cultural divide. Bernie Sanders is a socialist, pro-choice, and pro-same sex marriage progressive, representing the liberal Northeast. Liberty University on the other hand, represents the conservative, Evangelical and fundamentalist Christian south.

In a time where there is radical political and cultural polarization in America wherein there is very little true dialogue between the political left and right in this country, Bernie Sanders speaking engagement flipped the script and allowed us to see how true dialogue and exchange should occur.

Yet, there are many from the right and left who believe Sanders chapel message at Liberty University was the worst sort of compromise. There are those on the progressive left who believe Sanders had no business speaking and interacting with a segment of the American population that is against a woman's right to choose and for gays and lesbians to marry.

On the other hand, there are vocal people on the Evangelical and political right who believe Liberty University has sold its soul to political expediency by giving a pro-choice, pro-gay marriage and socialist politician a platform to spread heretical views that are entirely antithetical to Biblical Christianity.

It must be remembered, however, that Liberty University is not a church, but an institution of higher learning that is attempting to educate young people on how to engage the world around them. I personally applaud Liberty for inviting Sanders to speak. Having been partially educated in conservative and Evangelical Christian schools, I know all too well the intense criticism that Liberty University is currently receiving from some of its fundamentalist Christian brethren.

There are many within Liberty University's own Evangelical and fundamentalist tradition that believe that a school such as Liberty is only for the indoctrination of its students in its own tradition and that it must encourage the complete separation from alleged infidels such as the progressive Sanders.

Much of the Evangelical antagonism towards Sanders appearance at Liberty University has its roots in the old Fundamentalist and Modernist controversies of the 1920's where a massive and cataclysmic cultural and religious divide occurred around the Scopes Monkey Trial and other important divisive events. Since that time, fundamentalist Evangelical Christians and Liberal progressives have had little contact and even less cultural rapprochement.

Many in the Evangelical movement that Liberty University is a part of view Bernie Sanders as an interloper into their fundamentalist Zion and doubt that such engagement with the left has any positive advantage. They see Sanders as part of the Liberal elite who thumb their noses at and look down upon conservative Evangelicals as being obstructionist wackos.

However, I believe that Bernie Sanders appearance at Liberty University was not an appearance of the devil himself and does not compromise his progressive convictions. Nor does it violate Liberty University's educational mission to instruct students within an Evangelical and Biblical Christian worldview.

In all actuality, Liberty University's invitation and Sanders speaking engagement at Liberty is in keeping with the best of a true liberal arts education where interaction with a wide variety of viewpoints is seen as a tool of worldview formation. How can one disagree with a view they have actually never heard or interacted with personally?

Liberty University, while still a very conservative Evangelical institution, has a tradition of inviting contrarian guests as evidenced by allowing liberal Senatorial stalwart Teddy Kennedy to address the student body in the 1980's and permitting Virginia Governor Terry McAuliffe, a Democrat, to address the same student body last year.

Also, Liberty University has a unique ministry in America in which they give major political figures a platform to speak as a part of their educational and academic mission. Liberty should be applauded for developing diversity in our polarized world.

I believe a way for true progress to occur in America is if the polar right and the polar left attempt to come to the middle to seek some sort of commonality. Bernie Sanders appearance at Liberty University did that very thing and America is the better because of it.

Jesus Christ died on the cross and rose again from the dead to give eternal life to those who repent and believe in Him. He also said," go into the world and preach the gospel to every person." Liberty did that in inviting Bernie Sanders to speak in chapel. By bringing in Bernie Sanders to speak, Liberty University has shared the love of Christ with Sanders and the progressive world.

Thoughts on Ann Coulter

As one who has made a solemn vow to defend the nation of Israel and the Jewish people, I am now calling for the banishment of Ann Coulter from America's conservative movement, since there is no room in it for anti-Semitism and racism.

While I have not been a fan of Ann Coulter and her inflammatory brand of innuendo and invective sensationalism, this time she has crossed the line into clear hatred of Jewish people. Because of this, I would like to argue that Coulter's career as the shock princess of the hard right should come to an end.

Specifically, I am referring to her tweet yesterday in which she recklessly said, "How many f—ing Jews do these people think there are in the United States?"

For too long American conservatives have allowed Ms. Coulter, the pariah of conservatism to roam our movement without accountability. That ends now. I for one am calling for Ann Coulter's outright banishment for Republican and Conservative forums of any kind. Those who do not reject Ann Coulter are enabling an avowed enemy of the Jewish people.

I understand that Ms. Coulter has become rich and famous through her nonsensical brand of rabble – rousing and goading, but enough is enough.

It's high time to kick Ann Coulter to the curb and straight out of the conservative movement.

Carly Fiorina is no Fluke but Has Never Won an Election

I watched and re-watched last night's CNN's Presidential Debate and here are my thoughts on this highly entertaining venue.

Clearly the winner of last night's debate was Carly Fiorina, case closed. Only those partial to their particular candidate would say otherwise. While I personally will not be voting for her, she proved to the world again last night she is very gifted at debate. She was poised, articulate and very much on her game. Her comments on Planned Parenthood grabbed my attention.

However, despite Carly's amazing showing last night, I am left wondering why she did not win her race with Senator Boxer a few years ago. Before some of you jump on the Fiorina bandwagon, I think it is important to note that she has never won an election at the local or statewide level and that will be a problem for the GOP if it should choose Fiorina as the Republican nominee in 2016.

There is something about Carly Fiorina that I like. She kind of reminds me of the late Margaret Thatcher of England. Fiorina is one tough woman. She is a powerful force to be reckoned with for sure.

However, unlike Donald Trump and Ben Carson, the other two unexperienced politicians running for the Republican nomination, Carly Fiorina has ran for higher office and lost bad. This is important to note in choosing a candidate for President. The person we Republicans choose for our nominee should have a proven record of being able to win an election and despite her amazing talents; Carly Fiorina has not proven she can win any election at all.

Other Thoughts on the CNN Debate

Donald Trump's clown car continues down the road towards oblivion. It is obvious that Trump does not have the personal temperament to be President of the United States as Senator Rand Paul pointed out. Trump's attack on a US Senator's looks was not becoming of a potential leader of the free world.

While I am on the subject of Rand Paul, I have to admit that I wish CNN would have let him and Mike Huckabee have more time. Rand Paul has a lot of good things to say as his comments about engaging China and Russia point out. I am left wondering if Paul will ever get the chance to say more than a few brief comments.

Ben Carson's performance last night was not very good. While he is a gifted surgeon and great person, he is not that talented of a politician or public speaker. I went away from last night's debate wondering what all the fuss is about Ben Carson. I know he is almost a perfect saint of a person, but if we are honest it seems he that he needs to hone up on his public policy. Again, as in the case with Trump and Carly Fiorina, Ben Carson has absolutely no experience in politics and getting elected. I just don't think Ben Carson is ready at this level yet.

Jeb Bush did a little better than his Fox News debate performance. He still seems uncomfortable up there.

Ted Cruz on the other hand, is ready. He is also a gifted speaker. I believe Ted Cruz's comments on the Iran nuclear deal were among the most important and poignant. Cruz is spot on about this horrible deal with the terrorism supporting Iran. I believe that Cruz will be proven right about the colossal mistake that is this current nuclear agreement with Iran.

Marco Rubio also stood out last night. Marco is clearly a cut above most of the other candidates. In any other election year, Rubio would be at the top of the polls. But this is a highly unusual election cycle where outsiders like Carson, Fiorina and the Donald lead the pack because they are not part of the Washington machine.

Mike Huckabee has some good points about the clerk down in Kentucky and I wish, like the case of Rand Paul, that he would have been allowed more time. Huckabee clearly has a gift of connecting with others and I can understand why he was a highly successful pastor before he was the two term governor of Arkansas.

I am not a fan of Chris Christie, but I have to admit he was on his game last night. He was funny, likeable, and deft at connecting with his audience. However, there is no way in hades that I would ever vote for Chris Christie.

Scott Walker seemed to be off his game last night. I think it's time for him to wrap it up. John Kasich, along with Chris Christie, is probably my least favorite candidate running for President. He does not interest me at all.

All in all, it was Carly Fiorina's big night and she showed the world that she is a prime time player in this game of thrones.

How Paul Can Shock the World and Get Back into the Race

Tonight is a big night for the GOP. Weeks have passed since Megyn Kelly's line of questioning offended Donald Trump at the Fox News debate. Tonight is the CNN Republican primary debate and while the stakes are high for all the candidates, none can be higher than those of Senator Rand Paul.

While Paul has been lagging near the bottom of every important political poll, all that can change if Paul can catch lightning in the proverbial bottle and show the watching world why he is the candidate with the best ideas in this election cycle. All it takes is a major moment between Rand Paul and Donald Trump before millions of people tonight, and Paul can catapult himself right back to the forefront.

Rand Paul and his campaign know the seriousness of the matter and are going all out in preparation for tonight's CNN debate by buying commercial air time throughout the debate. Time will tell if Rand Paul's strategy will work and launch his trajectory, but tonight could be the start of something big. Ben Carson changed the trajectory of the race during the Fox News debate with a good debate performance and Rand Paul can do the same tonight.

Through the annals of presidential debate history one great or bad debate performance has changed the course of a Presidential election cycle. Case in point, in 1960, the American people took notice of a young senator named John F. Kennedy when he did very well in his televised debates with Richard Nixon. On the flip side, Gerald Ford's dismal performance against an unknown Georgia peanut farmer turned governor named Jimmy Carter embarrassed himself and was a determining factor in Carter's ascendency to the U.S. Presidency.

Tonight can be a game changer if Rand Paul can expose Donald Trump as the unexperienced political novice he really is. Trump's recent radio interview with conservative pundit Hugh Hewitt demonstrates that he has a glaring weakness in knowing essential people and power brokers throughout the world. All eyes will be on Donald Trump and Rand Paul can expose him as a fraud before the watching world.

Rand Paul can turn this race upside down if he does well in a toe to toe matchup with his nemesis Donald Trump. Stay tuned, it's about to get heavy in here. Donald Trump did not even want Rand Paul on the stage tonight and Trump could crumple before the world if Paul gets his chance.

Why Politics Matter

We live in an age of rampant cynicism. Many people are skeptical and angry at the institutions of government. Recent polling shows unequivocally that the vast majority of Americans have a bad opinion of what our politicians do in Washington.

The last poll I checked showed that less than 10% of Americans approve of Congress right now. With this low opinion of congress and the political system in America, the question may be rightly asked, does really politics matter after all?

I would answer this question in the affirmative since "politics" ultimately is the study of how people relate with other people. Like it or not, none of us can escape the subject of politics and human beings with government. Politics also deals with the subject of who holds power in a respective society and what rights individuals possess in that society.

It is undeniable reality that every society has laws and people who make those laws. While there are people who argue for a lawless society or anarchism, very few societies in the history of the world have existed where there were no laws to govern the actions and activities of individuals within a respective society or association of people.

While certain individuals and groups of people have attempted to live without laws, such antinomian experiments almost universally fail due to reality of humanities fallen nature. That is, society needs laws to prevent people from doing bad things.

One may question to veracity of my bleak estimation of human nature, but a quick and cursory examination of every day human relationships conclusively demonstrate that human beings left uncheck will do bad and dishonest things to each other.

While you might question my thesis that laws are necessary because people almost undoubtedly will do bad things if unchecked, it is unavoidable and empirically provable. Take for example, the mundane existence of car and house keys. In almost every civilization on earth keys exist to keep people from stealing things or entering into spaces that they do not own. If human beings are essentially good and trustworthy, why do almost all of us own keys to our homes and cars?

Yet, there is something even more universal about the existence of ordinary house and car keys. That is, underlying our keys is the notion of the laws that govern society. The keys that lock people in and out of their homes and cars can only prevent intruders to a certain point. If a person applies enough brute force or ingenuity, he or she can break into a domicile or automobile and circumvent the preventive purpose of keys.

However, every civilization has underlying laws and law enforcement that guarantee the sacrosanct nature of personal property. That is, if an individual chooses to circumvent and bypass the purpose of house and car keys and breaks into that domicile or car, the reality of the coercive power of the state and its laws will come into effect. That is, if a person chooses to break into another person's home or car, every society has laws to punish the thief and interloper. Without such laws that protect citizens from theft, violation and violence, society would most certainly crumble.

Simply put, every society on the face of the earth has a political and governing structure that makes laws that govern people. Similarly, every society ensures that this political and governing structure has the coercive power to punish individuals from violating the laws of a respective society.

While it is a reality that every society and civilization on the face of the earth has a political and governing structure that has the coercive power and authority to create laws and punish transgressive individuals with retribution for breaking the laws of a respective society.

However the reality of the existence of society, laws, and lawbreakers does not answer the question of who should make and enforce law in a respective society or civilization. As Jonathan Wolff writes in his insightful work, An

Introduction to Political Philosophy, "It has been said that there are only two questions in political philosophy: 'who gets what? and 'says who?'"

Furthermore, Wolff insightfully illustrates; "if someone has legitimate political power over me then they have the right to force me to do certain things. But how could another person justify the claim to have such rights over me."

In other words, how did the persons in power in a respective society get there and why do they have the right to enforce laws that govern my behavior and actions?

Throughout the annals of human history, philosophers, thinkers and astute observers of human civilization have pondered the nature of politics and have attempted to put forth respective systems of government to oversee the actions and activities of human beings.

Some of these systems and theories of government have been of a democratic and egalitarian nature; others have constructed more authoritarian, hierarchical, and oligarchical forms of government. Some of these systems of government have attempted to give men and women freedom; others have attempted to subjugate the citizens of a given society under the arbitrary and repressive laws of an elite few.

Cases in point, there have been some monarchs and dictators throughout history that believe that a god or gods have given them the unquestioned right to rule a people by fiat decree.

Thus, to answer the initial question I raised at the onset of this treatise, politics matters because the way people are governed matter. It is my belief that the best government is the least amount of government. I also believe the best government is the one who gives that safeguard the most liberty for its people. Politics matters because people need to be as free as possible to make the best choices for their own lives without coercion and fear.

On Ben Carson

There are interesting developments transpiring presently in the quest for the Republican Presidential Nomination. Recent polling demonstrates that former Neurosurgeon Dr. Ben Carson is now running neck and neck with real estate mogul Donald Trump

Carson, the former head of pediatric neurosurgery at Johns Hopkins and a longtime resident of Baltimore County, announced his candidacy for the 2016 GOP presidential nomination a few months ago in Detroit and is now surging nationally.

By all accounts Dr. Carson is a nice guy who loves God and loves his country. The Yale University and Michigan graduate is a gifted man and it is incredibly difficult for this commentator to say anything negative against him. However, it's important to note that Carson is not the conservative candidate many people have him out to be.

Ben Carson was the first surgeon to successfully separate conjoined twins joined at the head. In 2008, he was awarded the Presidential Medal of Freedom by President George W. Bush.

After delivering a widely publicized speech at the 2013 National Prayer Breakfast, he became a popular conservative figure in political media for his views on social and political issues.

Yet, if the discerning conservative voter takes a closer look at Carson's views, he or she might not like what they see.

Gun Control: Carson infamously told Glenn Beck "It depends on where you live. I think if you live in the midst of a lot of people, and I'm afraid that that semi-automatic weapon is going to fall into the hands of a crazy person, I would rather you not have it."

Minimum Wage: Carson believes that the federal minimum wage needs to be raised, despite the fact that he wrote in his own hand that raising the minimum wage will not fix income inequality.

Oil Prices and Ethanol Subsidies: Carson wants to redirect existing oil company subsidies towards ethanol subsidies instead despite claiming to be against all subsidies.

The Constitution: Carson has a unique interpretation of the separation of powers.

According to the Baltimore Sun, Carson says the United States should rethink the notion that a president must enforce laws the Supreme Court declares constitutional.

Carson said Sunday that "we need to discuss" the court's long-held power to review laws passed by Congress. That authority was established in the 1803 landmark case Marbury v. Madison.

While Ben Carson is a lot better candidate and person than Donald Trump, many of his views are far from being pristine and conservative.

Why You Should Vote for Rand Paul

Over the last few months I have been very vocal in my support of Rand Paul and this is why I now endorse him in his quest for the Presidency of the United States.

To many, 2016 may seem to a long way off. Why, "that's four months away" you might want to say. In reality, four months is just a blink of the eye. Soon, one of the most important election cycles in America's history will be in full swing and the stakes could not be any higher.

One may be skeptical about the importance of the coming Presidential election and think that one individual in the White House cannot effect much. Think again, if the last seven years teach us anything, the Obama years demonstrate unequivocally that one singular President can transform society.

Like him or leave him, President Barack Obama has fundamentally changed American society as we know it. Due to this present administration's massive overspending, the national debt now soars over $18 trillion dollars.

America presently spends approximately $7 million dollars per minute and this current spending spree cannot go on forever. Our crushing national debt, while not being taken seriously by Obama and his spend crazy friends in Washington, is not sustainable.

We need common sense solutions to face the crisis of our national debt head on. This is why Senator Rand Paul's proposal of adopting a Balanced Budget Amendment (BBA) for our Federal Government is both wise and prudent.

Throughout America 46 different states have enacted a Balanced Budget Amendment in their state constitutions. I concur with Senator Paul that the Federal Government must do the same.

I also agree with Senator Paul's plan for a $2 trillion dollar tax cut that will repeal the entire IRS tax code and replace it with a low, broad-based tax of a simple 14.5 percent on individuals and businesses.

While Rand Paul was not a member of the United States Senate during the 111th Congress, he states clearly that he would have voted against Obamacare and if elected President in 2016, one of his first acts in office would to be to repeal this grave injustice to our nation's health care system.

Equally appalling is our nation's crisis in relation to illegal immigration. Senator Rand Paul is correct when he says that illegal immigration places a massive drain on our economy and threatens our national security. He is prudent to call for the completion of a border fence in five years.

Senator Paul is also spot on when he calls for a complete and thorough audit of the Federal Reserve. Rand Paul is right when he says the Fed should be audited and the regulatory power should be placed back under the control of the United States Congress.

Similarly, we have a crisis in America over the bulk collection of our personal data from every American who owns a cell phone. We need a President who will guarantee our Constitutional right to privacy. As Senator Paul has said, the phone records of law-abiding Americans is none of the government's business.

As a Republican with distinctly Libertarian views on economics and civil liberties I agree with Rand Paul that individuals are sovereign over their own lives and that respect for privacy and individuals is the essential foundation for a free and prosperous world. Without liberty people become slaves to the State.

It is now a few months away from Republican primary season and Senator Rand Paul of Kentucky faces seeming insurmountable odds in wrestling the presidential nomination away from the likes of Donald Trump, Jeb Bush, and some of the other leading Republican candidates.

Part of the problem for Rand Paul comes from opposition within his own Party. Some important Republicans in congress and the U.S. Senate have resisted Rand Paul's pro-civil liberties stances.

Chief among Paul's main opponents in congress is Peter King, U.S. Representative for New York's 2nd Congressional district.

This past summer Rep. King refused to apologize for posting a tweet that linked Senator Paul to the terrorist organization known as ISIS or Islamic State.

King was upset about Rand Paul's opposition to the Patriot Act and the NSA's highly controversial phone-snooping program.

New Jersey Governor Chris Christie has made similar attacks against Rand Paul as evidenced by the fact that during the heated exchange between Christie and Paul during the Fox News Republican debate a few weeks ago, Christie made the claim that Paul would be responsible for the next terrorist attack on American soil due to his opposition to the NSA.

In face of these constant attacks against Rand Paul, many of which are sadly coming from his own party, it is of paramount importance that those of us who support Rand's presidential bid be cognizant of this opposition and be able to defend Paul's positions on national security and opposition to terrorism.

As Senator Paul clearly stated in his winning exchange with the outmatched Chris Christie, he is not opposed to taking a strong stand for our nation's security, he just does not want to violate our Constitutional rights in the process.

I concur with Rand Paul that we must be strong against the onslaught against ISIS and other national security threats while preserving our civil liberties as delineated by the U.S. Constitution.

While I agree we must be diligent against terror, we must not relinquish our Constitutional rights to the Federal Government which clearly does not have our best interests at heart.

The Left's Hidden War against Conservative America

One of the most influential novels to emerge in Evangelical circles during the last quarter of the 20th Century was *This Present Darkness* by Frank Peretti. Published in 1986 by Crossway Books, *This Present Darkness* discusses the power of prayer and the hidden world of angels, demons and spiritual warfare.

To date, *This Present Darkness* has sold in excess of 2.5 million copies worldwide and remained on the Christian Booksellers Association top best sellers list for over 150 consecutive weeks after its release.

This Present Darkness takes its title from Ephesians 6:12, which says, "For we do not wrestle against flesh and blood, but against the rulers, against the authorities, against the cosmic powers over this present darkness, against the spiritual forces of evil in the heavenly places."

The essential thesis of *This Present Darkness* is that there is a hidden spiritual world of darkness and demons that must be overcome by vigilant prayer.

Presently there is also a political battle for the soul of America. We might not see or believe we are experiencing this battle, but it is all around us and affects each and everyone one of us.

The battle I am referring to pertains to the left's war on Middle America and its conservative values.

Many of the educated cultural elites in the country believe in the thesis articulated by the Ancient Greek philosopher Plato, who in his *Republic* argued against Democracy and the participation of the common people (polis) in the political affairs of Athens. Plato believed that only the ruling class of philosopher kings should have a say in the rule of a respective nation.

While the progressive left does not want say this in public, but many leftists and collectivists have appropriated Plato's undemocratic mindset and believe that the educated left alone is fit to govern in the United States. An unspoken class warfare and caste system has arisen between the liberal "cultural elites" and conservative Middle America.

You may not see this see this class warfare on the surface level, but if you probe and investigate what the left is saying about conservatives in this country, you will find that it is insulting and disparaging.

Many of people on the left openly laugh at the notion of our Constitutional rights and believe that America should be ruled arbitrarily by the collective consensus of political correctness.

Case in point, on the issue of the 2nd Amendment, you need to know that many people on the left do not believe rank and file conservatives should be able to determine for ourselves if we should own a firearm or rifle. Despite what the U.S. Constitution says, the left believes it is superior to this storied foundational document itself.

The left ultimately believes it knows what is best for you and me. Similarly, the left believes you and I are not qualified to make rational decisions about gun ownership and wants to take our rights and guns away.

You need to know about the left's war upon conservative Middle America. It rages all around us and you will find it if you have eyes to see.

Rand Paul is the True Reformer

Anyone that is paying close attention to the current political situation in America can tell you that our political system is broken.

Recent polling shows that the vast majority of Americans have a radically low opinion of what is currently transpiring in Washington and the approval ratings of Congress is tragically at an all-time low.

What Congress actually does puzzles many of us. While Congress spends and appropriates billions of our hard earned money on their alleged new legislation, nothing seems to get done each and every year.

When Congress and our ineffectual President do act, it is always in their own interests and contrary to our personal freedom and civil liberties. While the national debt now rests at close to $19 trillion dollars, America is none the better in proportion to the vast sums of money being spent.

The resultant effect of this dismal performance of our elected officials has meant disastrous ruin for our country as a whole. Our economy is weak, illegal immigration is a major national problem and our city streets are spiraling out of control with murder and violence.

How did this happen? What caused this disastrous political climate in America and what can be done to rectify it?

We Must Reject Entitlements and Turn to Free Enterprise

Since the enactment of the New Deal legislation and Great Society legislation of Franklin Delano Roosevelt and Lyndon Johnson, many Americans have looked to the federal government to meet their basic needs.

Instead of being weaned off government assistance and entitlements, progressive social reforms and legislation has created life-long servitude and dependence on government assistance.

This wholesale dependency upon government has given rise to the monstrosity that is present day Washington. It is now almost impossible for real change to occur in our highest echelon of government because those being enriched by tax payer money do not want to change the system or relinquish power to those who truly want to fix our broken political and economic system.

The kings and power brokers of Washington want to ride this gravy train and vicious cycle as long as they can and will attempt with great vehemence to thwart any real change.

This is why true political reformers like Rand Paul are opposed by both the mainstream media and the political establishment of both major parties. It is unbridled greed for money and power that primes the pump of the political machine that is present day Washington.

In order to slay the dragon that is our bloated government, a new generation of dragon slayers must arise to kill the steely beast.

Unless there is fundamental change in Washington, the same old game of thrones is going to happen year, year after year.

A revolution needs to take place throughout America that informs our citizens that for true freedom to occur, Washington must be reformed, downsized and brought under control. True freedom means independence from government control and subsidy. Self-determinism and personal empowerment through free market enterprise is the only way to go.

True political reform is possible in America if true citizen patriots, dedicated to liberty, try to enact it.

Rand Paul Can Still Win the Nomination

Call me a dreamer, but I still believe that Rand Paul can shake off these bad poll numbers and become a viable contender for the Republican nomination next year and here's how.

Admittedly, it will be a herculean task for Libertarian leaning Senator from Kentucky, but dim prospects notwithstanding, there is still a nominating pathway for Rand Paul. As his win in the most recent straw poll demonstrates, Rand Paul still has many supporters.

It will take a spark, perhaps a winning debate performance akin to Carly Fiorina's amazing showings in the first two Republican debates. Something tells me that Rand Paul has one such sterling performance in him.

The time is ripe for Rand Paul to make his ascendency because this race is still in radical flux right now as demonstrated by the climb and fall of Ben Carson in recent weeks and the fact that Fiorina now sits in the second place slot in the polls behind Donald Trump, whose polls numbers have dipped considerably since their stratosphere reaching peak a month ago.

Many pundits and astute observers of this chaotic race believe that the Donald has peaked and may have lost a lot of steam because of his inconsistent debate performances and constant and unnecessary personal attacks as demonstrated during CNN's Republican Primary debate held at the Reagan Library in Simi Valley, California.

If Rand Paul can have dramatic debate performance like Carly Fiorina or do something absolutely news busting on the floor or the U.S. Senate, he can get back in this race at the right time and climb the charts faster than Taylor Swift's "1989."

All it takes is a spark.

Republicans and Libertarians can work Together

Bob Dylan, the iconic folk-rock star famously crooned in his archetypal 1960's protest song, "The Times They Are a-Changin." American society, midway into the second decade of the new millennium, is certainly changing. In reality,

American society is in such a radical state of free fall and flux that it would be hardly recognizable to generations of previous Americans.

We live in a time period of American history where liberal and counter cultural values have gone mainstream, gained ascendency and reshaped the very social fabric of American civilization.

From the passage of the Affordable Health Care Act (Obamacare) to the Supreme Court's redefinition of marriage in this year's Supreme Court ruling in Obergefell vs. Hodges, American civilization has been fundamentally changed by Barack Obama and his progressive cohorts' liberal activism.

For those of us who are of a conservative and Libertarian mindset, there could be a tendency to retreat in our own subcultures, places of worship and focus groups and abandon any attempt to impact and transform America through our own values.

I for one want to resist this tendency, all too common within American conservatism, to retreat and abandon mainstream society. In fact, I am doing everything in my power for us conservatives and Libertarians to shun retreat and defeatism.

Because we are often outnumbered in collective society, I am presently advocating a form of detente, or easing of hostility and division amongst small government and pro-civil liberties Republicans and Libertarians. I believe there is much common ground between these ideological and political camps and that rather than focusing on the issues that divide us, let us unite by emphasizing the many things we agree on.

America is too great and life is too short for those of us with such similar views to be divided. Both small government Republicans and Libertarians can agree on the fact that the federal government is presently far too big, intrusive, costly and expansive.

We can also agree on the fact that the $18 trillion dollar national debt is unsustainable and unviable for America's future. I believe we can work together for common economic and political causes for the good of America. Please consider joining me. I have just started a whole new organization called, "Republicans and Libertarians United." Join me in working together with Republicans and Libertarians across America for common economic and political causes.

Why Liberty Matters

As Americans, we are familiar with the word "liberty." The term is an important part of the social and political fabric of American society. Patrick Henry's famous statement, "give me liberty or give me death" are meaningful words to most Americans. "My country 'tis of Thee, sweet land of liberty" are words from a song most of us have at least heard once in our lifetime. But what is "liberty" really? We Americans speak and sing of "liberty" all the time.

The English word "liberty" is derived from the Latin term *liber*, which means to "free one's self." Philosophically speaking, liberty is the quality individuals have to control their own actions. From time immemorial philosophers, sages and astute observers of human have contemplated the concept of liberty.

The Apostle Paul wrote in the New Testament, "Now the Lord is the Spirit, and where the Spirit of the Lord is, there is liberty" (2 Corinthians 3: 17).

The Roman Emperor Marcus Aurelius, in the first chapter of his "Meditations" stated that liberty is "a polity in which there is the same law for all, a polity administered with regard to equal rights and equal freedom of speech, and the idea of a kingly government which respects most of all the freedom of the governed."

Thomas Hobbes in the second chapter of his classic work on political philosophy *Leviathan* wrote on the concept of liberty when he stated therein, "a free man is he that in those things which by his strength and wit he is able to do is not hindered to do what he hath the will to do."

The eminent thinker John Locke stated, "In the state of nature, liberty consists of being free from any superior power on Earth."

The famous Utilitarian philosopher John Stuart Mill, in his seminal work, *On Liberty* argued that liberty is the freedom to act with the absence of coercion.

Yet, while the concept of liberty has been featured prominently in the storied annals of American history, recent events and persons over the last decade have quickly eroded the concept of liberty in the United States.

If recent American history tells us anything, it demonstrates that we live in very tumultuous times. Recent news headlines are replete with accounts of violent crimes and deadly protests across America. From the mass shootings in Charleston, South Carolina to the surreal sight of armored military vehicles patrolling the streets of Ferguson, MO, America appears at times to be coming apart at the seams.

The Erosion of Freedom in American Politics and Government

In recent years this country has endured cataclysmic change in the area of politics and government as well. From the passing of 2010's Affordable Care Act (ACA) or colloquially Obamacare to Supreme Court's redefinition of marriage *Obergefell v. Hodges* this year, American society has been transformed by our socially progressive and leftist-activist government.

Anyone who thinks they can avoid the effects and reach of our transformative and ideology driven government needs to think again. Almost every activity and endeavor an American citizen is involved in these days is overtaxed and overregulated by the federal government.

We also have conclusive evidence that the federal government, under the guise of the Patriot Act, is spying on our cell phone calls and collecting data on our personal lives. From the food you eat and the clothes on your back, the government is also there to tax and regulate you. The long arm of the State is there to overtax your income, home and place of business.

Many people are passive about the federal government's activism and activities and do not care about the government's overreach in our personal and economic lives. They are resigned to the fact that the "man is going to stick it to us one way or another."

Even many conservative Christians in this country are ok with this present government's intrusion and intervention into our private and fiscal lives. Many Evangelicals I have encountered, argue that we are to "Render onto Caesar what is Caesar's" (Matthew 22:21 and Mark 12:17).

While I am a Bible believing Christian, I reject the servile attitude many Evangelical pastors have fostered in their congregants towards the federal government by implying that by "obeying the governing authorities" (Romans 13:1-7), we are not to fight against the federal government for any reason.

Yet, the last time I checked, America is a both a constitutional and participatory democracy of the people, by the people and for the people and that we are allowed by the U.S. Constitution to fight against laws we deem to be unjust.

In all actuality, I am arguing that a good citizen of this country should stand up and speak out against the excessive intrusion and expansion of the federal government into our personal lives.

Make no mistake about it my friends, this present Obama administration and the progressive left in this country has a fundamentally different view about Democracy. It believes that an elite few liberal activists alone should transform society. To many liberals to fight against Obama and the left's policies is tantamount to hate speech and violating political correctness.

I am arguing for freedom from the tyranny and overreach of the state. I am arguing against the idolatry of state worship and interdependence. I want you to live free or die hard.

Liberty matters my friend. Will you be free or a slave to the state?

After eight years of Obama wherein he recreated much of American society in his liberal image, it is doubtful that the United States, we Libertarians and conservatives have grown to love can be salvaged if Hillary Clinton or Bernie Sanders are elected President.

Yet, someone might say that things will change if Jeb Bush is elected President. Oh, Really? We gave his brother an eight year crack at it and that did not go so well, did it? Why would we want to give another Bush a shot and salvaging American when Jeb is using the same failed advisors his, W used?

The choice before us is clear. It is liberty or the tyranny of the state. If don't elect a man like Rand Paul who will most certainly work to end the national debt, restore our civil liberties and freedom and make massive changes in the very structure of American government, or it will be more of the same old thing. It will be the crying game for conservatives and libertarians all over again.

We who love and support Rand Paul can make a difference. If a few thousand of us banded together like the Spartans of 300, we can turn this entire election cycle on its head and help Rand Paul win. It will, however, take a force of will. It will take some dedicated supporters who are willing to give it their all to make the biggest difference of all. The choice is yours.

Answering the National Review's Attack on Rand Paul

(Here is the letter I send to the National Review in NYC. As a life-longer reader of NR, I have grown weary of NR's constant attacks on Ron and Rand Paul. Because they declined to print the following letter, I post here for your reading pleasure).

National Review
215 Lexington Ave, New York, NY 10016
August 21, 2015

Addressing NR's Mischaracterizations of Rand Paul
The inimitable G. K. Chesterton once offered this sagely observation; "The true soldier fights not because he hates what is in front of him, but because he loves what is behind him." Today I write about an apparent literary faux

pas and ad hominem perpetrated by various writers for NR, not because I eschew locking horns with some of the best writers in American conservatism, but because of NR's indelible impact on my past. In fact, I would be exceedingly remiss if I did not mention that Mr. Buckley and NR was not a pivotal instrument in my own intellectual development as a youth. NR and Mr. Buckley's Firing Line both made an indelible impact on me during my formidable years.

Yet, having said this, I would be equally indolent in my duties towards the same conservative movement NR so eloquently champions, if I did not suggest for your careful perusal, that NR is guilty of engaging in a sustained presuppositional bias against Senator Rand Paul of Kentucky. Forgive me for appropriating potentially idiosyncratic theoretical phraseology indigenous to the political thought of the late Dutch conservative and neo-Calvinist Abraham Kuyper, D. Vollenhoven and Herman Dooyeweerd, which has taught me to detect the underlying ideological reference point of a given argument.

It is apparent to this reader that NR has a discernable predisposition against Rand Paul and the Kentucky Senator's particular brand of Libertarianism. I would like to also suggest that this obvious precondition against Paul's almost Nozician minimal state ideology has caused some of your writers to lapse into some very clear logical fallacies and errors of judgment.

Case in point, in Andrew C. McCarthy's June 6 piece entitled, "Rand Paul's Faux-Libertarian Opposition to the Patriot Act," engages in true ad hominem and misrepresentation of Senator Paul's political philosophy when he suggests that Senator Paul aversion to the Patriot Act "camouflage his real objection," and that Senator Paul is in actuality, "anti-government in respect to national security."

Yet, not only does Mr. McCarthy cast unwarranted dispersion upon Senator Paul's views of government, but also engages in the straw man fallacy by attributing to Senator Paul a view that he does not in fact maintain. It is almost laughable that Mr. McCarthy suggests that Senator Paul is "anti-government" when Paul himself is an active participatory member of the highest echelon of American government itself. If Senator Paul was "anti-government" as Mr. McCarthy wrongly suggests, why then, has Senator Paul spent almost his entire life engaged in shaping American government itself? Mr. McCarthy may be correct in his assessment that he has a radically different view of the function of government than Rand Paul, but it is beneath his high calling as a writer of American conservatism's preeminent literary magazine to suggest that Paul's position is close to anarchism.

Sadly, Mr. McCarthy is not the only writer for NR that has engaged in *ad hominems* against Senator Paul's person and political positions. Tragically, Eliana Johnson, Fred Fleitz and Rich Lowry have been very unflattering towards Senator Paul and his father in the past as well. It appears from the vantage point of this life-longer reader, that NR sees itself as the ultimate gatekeeper and arbitrator of who should be deemed "orthodox" in the American conservative movement.

Sadly, many of the writers of NR are now mischaracterizing Senator Rand Paul in its litmus test crusade for ideological orthodoxy. These mischaracterizations of Senator Paul's political philosophy and policy positions are internally inconsistent and implode due to their utilizations of the logical fallacies of ad hominem, straw man and Red herring, and distract from the substantive issues facing America in one of the most important election cycles in our history.

Lee Edward Enochs
Princeton, NJ

With Trump Imploding, Time for Republicans to Turn to Paul

I knew Donald Trump could not resist shooting himself in the foot, but this is getting ridiculous. Just hours after Megyn Kelly returned from vacation, Trump unleashed a Twitter assault against her that demonstrates clearly what many of us long-time Republicans have known since Trump first announced that he is running for President; that he does not have the character or temperament for the job.

As Trump continues his slow implosion, it is time for the Republican Party faithful to start looking to other candidates that could actually win the Presidential election.

No one deserves a second look than Senator Rand Paul, the politician clearly with the most innovative ideas of the multiplicity of candidates running for President.

Giving Senator Paul a second look would be timely for Americans, especially as we face uncertain and unsettling economic news from Wall Street. Senator Paul is clearly the best and the brightest candidate of all the Republicans running and only Paul has a viable plan to balance the federal budget in five years and eliminate the $18 trillion dollar national debt.

It's time to stop playing games with America's future and turn the best and the brightest.

Donald Trump's traveling circus was wild and crazy while it lasted, but it's time to end play time and turn to a proven conservative like Rand Paul. Trump's daily implosion opens the door for Paul to climb in the polls and turn this election upside down.

Take Another Look at Rand Paul

As Donald Trump surges into the polling stratosphere, left behind are the conservative ideas that the Republican Party has been founded on. Sure, Donald Trump is brash and is appealing to a populist element within the Republican Party; his presentation is high on soundbites and devoid of substantive ideas.

I think it is time for the rank and file of the Republican Party that actually votes in the primaries to take another look at the ideas of Senator Rand Paul before settling on an unproven and unstable commodity like Donald Trump or a middle of the road questionable conservative like Jeb Bush.

While the Republican Party is supposed to be the place where conservative ideas flourish and gain ascendency, Trump's overall ideology is one garbled mess. This is an individual who unlike Rand Paul, has very recently supported high taxes, Obamacare and single-payer healthcare where one government run organization would collect all healthcare fees and pay out all healthcare costs.

Trump has also very recently been a Democrat that supported Hillary Clinton, gun control and partial birth abortion. Trump has been anything but a rock of consistence on conservative issues.

Rand Paul, on the other hand, has been a man of principle his entire adult life and has stood for true small-government and conservative values. Besides defending our civil liberties and advocating the abolition of the NSA, TSA, IRS and Patriot Act, Rand Paul, unlike any of the other candidates has a five year plan to balance the federal budget and eliminate our $19 trillion dollar national deficit.

Rand Paul, a medical physician by trade, has stood for pro-life issues his entire life and supports the defunding of Planned Parenthood because it comes from his belief system and personal conviction, not because it is the popular thing to do.

Before Republican waste another Presidential election cycle on a candidate that cannot win the general election like Donald Trump, we in the GOP need to look again to a true conservative like Rand Paul who can actually beat

Hillary Clinton by winning the swing states like Ohio, Pennsylvania, Colorado and Michigan as the polls indicate.

Fellow Conservatives, Libertarians and Republicans, don't waste your vote on Donald Trump! Take another look at Rand Paul; he is the conservative you have been looking for all along.

Take another look at Rand Paul. America is too great to throw away your vote on an unproven commodity…

The Coming Economic Collapse?

For many years former Congressman Ron Paul has been predicting the economic collapse of America.

Earlier this year Paul warned in television commercials of a calamitous U.S. financial crisis that could bring civil unrest and a stock market collapse—a crash "infinitely worse than the crisis of 2008.

Maybe Ron Paul is right after all.

Today was one of the worst days on Wall Street in recent memory.

Wall Street dropped on Monday in tumultuous action as traders raced into safe-haven assets amid mounting worries over instability in China and emerging markets.

The Dow Jones Industrial Average skidded 588.5 points, or 3.6%, to 15871.3.

Why this economic tumult does not spell the end of America as we know it, it does show how quickly things can turn for the United States.

One only has to recall the massive economic problems that befell America in 2008 and 1929 to demonstrate that America's economy could collapse in an instance due to our interdependence and interconnectivity with the world market.

I am mindful of the historical instance of the Sack of Rome which occurred on August 24, 410 A.D., exactly 1605 years ago today.

The Sack of Rome occurred on August 24, 410. The city was attacked by the Visigoths, led by Alaric I. At that time, Rome was no longer the capital of the Western Roman Empire, having been replaced in that position by Ravenna in 402. Nevertheless, the city of Rome retained a paramount position as "the eternal city" and a spiritual center of the Empire. The sack was a major shock to contemporaries, friends and foes of the Empire alike.

This was the first time in almost 800 years that Rome had fallen to a foreign enemy. The previous sack of Rome had been accomplished by the Gauls under their leader Brennus in 387 BC. The sacking of 410 is seen as a major landmark in the fall of the Western Roman Empire. St. Jerome, living in Bethlehem at the time, wrote that "The City which had taken the whole world was itself taken.

I bring up the historical occurrence of the Sack of Rome to demonstrate that a nation can fall in an instance and if America is not careful, it too could fall into absolute chaos.

Thoughts on the Gay Marriage Debate

As a conservative with a distinctly Libertarian perspective on the relationship between our free citizenry and the government, I have carefully researched the debate over same-sex marriage in America and believe there are some significant factors why social conservatives lost the gay marriage debate in the United States. While I am a traditionalist when it comes to marriage, these are my observations on why social conservatives ultimately lost the debate on marriage in society.

On June 26, 2015 American society changed forever. On that fateful Friday, the United States Supreme Court ruled in the landmark 5-4 Obergefell v. Hodges decision, that gay and lesbians have a fundamental right to marry by both the Due Process Clause and Equal Protection Clause of the Fourteenth Amendment to the United States Constitution.

Decided on June 26, 2015, *Obergefell v. Hodges* overturned *Baker* and requires all states to issue marriage licenses to same-sex couples and to recognize same-sex marriages validly performed in other jurisdictions. *Obergefell* v. *Hodges* states that same-sex couples have the same fundamental rights guaranteed to every other citizen by the U.S. Constitution. Same-sex marriage is now legal and the law of the land throughout the U.S. and its possessions and territories.

As a U.S. citizen with roots in both the conservative Evangelical and social conservative movements in this country, I am well aware of the outrage that many within

these movements have over the Supreme Court's
Obergefell v. Hodges ruling.

Yet, in the two months that has transpired since this
historic ruling, I have noticed inherent weaknesses in the
arguments those opposed to same-sex marriage are making
against Obergefell v. Hodges.

First of all, it has become very apparent to me that many
social conservatives are so angry about this verdict that
they cannot formulate calm and cognitive arguments
against it. Many of the opponents to *Obergefell v. Hodges*
I have encountered have engaged in internet flame wars
and shouting matches with those who support same-sex
marriage. Many opponents to gay marriage lose control of
their ability to argue dispassionately for their views and do
their cause irrevocable harm.

The second major weakness I have seen in social
conservative opposition to same-sex marriage is their
appeal to some sort of nebulous and ahistorical time period
where "America was a Christian nation." These opponents
of gay marriage argue that Obergefell v. Hodges
undermines the decided Christian intentions of the framers
of the U.S. Constitution, a spurious historical claim, since
Benjamin Franklin, Thomas Jefferson and many of the
other "Founding Fathers" were most definitely not
Christian in any traditional sense.

Many social conservatives have a distinctly Christian
understanding of the U.S. Constitution and interpret this
storied document from the framework of the Judeo-
Christianity. Yet, the First Amendment is very clear that
the laws of America are to remain entirely neutral in

matters of religion and the Fifth and Fourteenth Amendments possess a "due process" clause that guarantees that every American is to have equal access and protection under the law. The U.S. Constitution applies to every American irrespective if they are an Evangelical, Catholic, Social Conservative or none of the above.

Lastly, an egregious and fatal flaw of social conservative opposition to gay marriage is these movements seeming inability to give credence to the notion that gays and lesbians should have any rights at all. When questioning many conservative Evangelicals on what rights they believe gay and lesbian partners should have, many have rejoined, "none, because homosexuality is an abomination to God."

This sort of caustic rhetoric is unhelpful to those who believe same-sex couples should not have the right to marry under the law. It appears to border on fanaticism and bigotry to many Americans. Those opposed to same sex marriage have to explain why they believe some Americans do not deserve equal access and protection under the laws of the land. They also must explain carefully what rights they believe gay and lesbian partners should have if they should not be able to marry.

While questioning arguments fundamentalists made for traditional marriage in a bygone generation, most Americans came to the resolution that gay and lesbians should have the same rights and anybody else. Most Americans know at least one gay and lesbian person, deem them normal and believe they should not be relegated to second-class status under the law. Most Americans believe that gays and lesbians should be full participants in our Democratic process are not to be discriminated against by the laws of our land.

Social conservatives lost the gay marriage debate because they did not understand that American society passed them by. Yes, *Obergefell v. Hodges* was a very narrow decision, but many social conservatives refuse to identify the changing cultural and ideological landscape of contemporary American society.

Liberty and Autonomy

The famous playwright and literary critic T.S. Eliot once wrote, "Only those who will risk going too far can possibly find out how far one can go."

 I think I know something of what the preeminent Harvard educated essayist meant. That is, I know what it is like to risk it all and go as far as one can go.

While I do not often speak of a dark chapter in my life, I think I can share that there was a time in my life about a decade ago, where I was so burned out on the American status quo that I decided to abandon normative American civilization for the idyllic and rural beaches of the North Shore of Oahu, Hawaii. For over a year, I lived in virtual isolation from friends and family as I contemplated the meaning of human existence.

I also know something of the existential and spiritual crisis the British author Somerset Maugham wrote about in his classic novel, *The Razor's Edge.* I have been to edge of human existence and looked deeply into the abyss of self-contemplation that the famed iconoclast Friedrich Nietzsche warned of when he quipped, "Beware of looking too long into the abyss for the abyss will look back into you."

Yet, after looking into the abyss, I came out better and stronger because of it. I came away from what many astute theologians call, "the dark night of the soul." For during that 12 month "walk on the wild side," I came to the bottom of what I really believe about life, love, and the essence of reality.

From that period of contemplation and utter disillusionment with the bankruptcy of contemporary American culture, I came out a stronger Christian with a robust faith in the orthodox Christian view of Jesus Christ and formulated my own personal and political philosophy. I came back from the brink with a philosophy of Libertarian autonomy.

I now believe it was God who helped me realize the meaning of human autonomy and I now advocate a conception of individualism that stresses a radical independence from the external world and its political and ecclesial sociological structures. I now believe that the best government is the least amount of government and that we as human beings are most fulfilled when we free from dependence on anything except ourselves.

As a proponent of a radical Libertarian view of self-sufficiency, I cannot tolerate the government attempting to micro-manage my economic, sexual, spiritual and political life. Because of this, I cannot tolerate any political candidate or ideologue who maintains collectivism and centralized government. This is why out of all the candidates running for President, I can only support Rand Paul. The Republican Senator from Kentucky is the only candidate that cares about our true independence from the State. For this reason, I am voting and campaigning for Rand Paul.

Thoughts on Donald Trump

 "I crashed my car into a bridge and I don't care" -Icona Pop

At the risk of seeming implacable and impenitent, I have to confess to you, that I just don't care about Donald Trump.

Sure, I would like to have a fraction of the $8 billion dollars he has accumulated as a real estate mogul and male reality television diva, but other than my immediate capital gain, I don't care.

Call me heartless or even worse, call me indifferent, but I simply don't care that the magnanimous Donald J. Trump is playing America like a one string banjo down in the bayous.

The man is an imposter on the American political stage and he is playing the media and his legion of mindless drones who buy into his spurious hagiography.

The gravamen or central point in my complaint against Trump is that Donald J. simply does not care either.

Donald Trump just does not care that he is making a flying mockery of the political landscape in America.

I am simply disinterested in Trump and his followers, like a moth to a flame, they will be around for a quick second and will crash and burn when they get too close to the fire of the media's scrutiny.

When I look at Trump and his legions, I simply don't care.

Why I am Taking a Stand for Rand Paul

"If I profess, with the loudest voice and the clearest exposition, every portion of the truth of God except precisely that little point which the world and the devil are at that moment attacking, I am not confessing Christ, however boldly I may be professing Christianity. Where the battle rages the loyalty of the soldier is proved; and to be steady on all the battle-field besides is mere flight and disgrace to him if he flinches at that one point"

Martin Luther (1483-1546)

Just moments ago I send my proposed op/ed essay to American conservatism's most respected periodical. I have read this magazine my entire life and I am not sure where I would be at without it. This formidable vehicle of literary output made an indelible impact on my own personal life.

Yet, despite this magazine's considerable influence on my life, I believe it is dead wrong about Rand Paul. I believe it has engaged in many logical fallacies about Rand Paul's character and policy positions.

Why am I coming to the defense of Rand Paul? Because I am a true believer in Senator Paul's Presidential bid and views on government, reducing the national debt and defending our civil liberties.

I take this stand for Rand Paul at a considerable risk to my life and future. I run the risk of seeming like a conservative ideologue. I did not actually come to the city of Princeton in order to become a political leader. Yet, things have changed and I now believe one of my functions in life is to speak out for what is right in American politics.

I know that Rand Paul's views on politics and government go against grain of the Republican status quo. I do not care, like Martin Luther of old; I must take a stand for what I know is right and because my conscience knows is right.

Should Jon Stewart Moderate a Presidential Debate?

If you keep up with the latest comings and goings in the world of politics, but now you might have heard that a group of Jon Stewart fans are circulating a petition arguing that the former "Daily Show" comedian and liberal political pundit is "more than qualified" to moderate a Presidential Debate.

These diehard Stewart fans launched Change.org petition a couple of weeks ago, after the liberal television show host signed off for the final time as the helm of the *Daily Show*. They have asked the Commission on Presidential Debates to consider allowing the progressive Stewart to grill the presidential candidates in an upcoming debate in 2016. According to TIME Magazine, the petitioners now have over 100,000 signatures and are now 31,000 signers short of its 150,000 goal.

We conservatives should abhor the prospect of Jon Stewart moderating a coming primary or general election Presidential debate since Stewart has been anything but a friend to Republicans and conservatives in this country.

While Stewart and his drones love to toot their own horns and self-congratulate themselves for being "enlightened souls" and part of the "distracted middle," they are anything but.

Anyone who has watched the *Daily Show* knows that such claims of objectivity are an abject lie. Jon Stewart is a pawn of the level and his entire tenure on Comedy Central was a laugh fest against conservatives and Republicans in this country.

The *Atlantic* had an article back in February that showed conclusively that Jon Stewart has a liberal bias against conservatives. That article can be read here: http://www.theatlantic.com/entertainment/archive/2015/02/why-theres-no-conservative-jon-stewart/385480/

Jon Stewart is anything but objective in his political commentary and is a definite leftist with an agenda against conservatism in America. Despite claims of "neutrality" and "objectivity," Stewart is just a liberal hack who likes his comedic flunkies Stephen Colbert, John Oliver and *Daily Show* replacement Trevor Noah.

To allow Jon Stewart to moderate and host a presidential debate in 2016 would be a travesty and something the Republican Party and conservatives across this country should not tolerate.

Thoughts on Ron Paul on His 80th Birthday

Today is former Congressman and Presidential Candidate Ron Paul's 80th birthday. Out of commemoration of this great man's eight-fold octennial celebration, I thought it would be fitting for me to write an essay about how Ron Paul's weighty ideas have profoundly changed my life.

I have not always been the enthusiastic Libertarian that many of you observe today. In fact, for most of my life I have been sort of a social conservative and establishment type Republican and toed the party line on just about everything.

While I have known about Ron Paul at least since 1988, when he ran for President as a member of the Libertarian Party. Congressman Paul was trounced by the Bush / Quayle ticket that year, getting a grand total of 432,179 votes (0.5%).

Despite his relative cultural and political obscurity, Ron Paul's Libertarianism remained intriguing to me over the years. Perhaps it was my vigorous interaction with devout Libertarians and Ayn Rand disciples on the various college campuses I ministered at Southern California, I am not exactly sure why.

Despite my respect for Ron Paul's desire for the passage of a balanced budget amendment and small government ideas, I kept my distance from Paul and his disciples over the years because they seemed like radical obstructionists out to unsettle the apple cart of the Republican Party.

However, my thoughts about Ron Paul and his Libertarian ideology started to change during and in the aftermath of George W. Bush's disastrous war in Iraq, which cost the American tax payer over $2 trillion dollars and caused hundreds of thousands of people to tragically lose their lives for no apparent good reason.

My disillusionment with Bush over the Iraq war allowed me to look elsewhere for new ideas within American conservatism. In my ample studies of political philosophy and economics, I came full circle to a Libertarian position very similar to that of Ron Paul.

I no longer believe that America should be the world's policeman and no longer believe we should attempt to right every wrong and fight every battle that transpires across the globe.

Ron Paul also has greatly influenced me to defend my civil liberties, distrust and question the federal reserve, Patriot Act, TSA, NSA, IRS, foreign aid to hostile nations and believe that unless America deals with our $18 trillion dollar national debt we might not survive as a nation.

It was some militant disciples of Ron Paul down in Texas that finally pushed me over the edge. These zealous libertarian and Ron Paul acolytes helped me realize that America is a nation predicated upon the U.S. Constitution and for this I want to thank Congressman Paul for his often unpopular efforts to save America. For these efforts I want to wish him a happy birthday. While he did not win the Presidency, he sure won me over to his Libertarian vision for America.

Conservatives Must Be Active in the Political Arena or America is Doomed to Destruction by Rampant Liberalism

Creed- (also confession, symbol, or statement of faith) is a statement of the shared beliefs of a religious community in the form of a fixed formula summarizing core

I have enjoyed an unusual summer. Several months ago, as a graduate student here on the East Coast, this conservative found himself in unfamiliar waters, so I started to film in various locations around the Princeton, New Jersey area with my iPad. These videos are usually accompanied with my running commentary on various political issues and current events transpiring in America. Altogether several thousand people have viewed these Libertarian-leaning conservative videos. Because I have decidedly Libertarian and conservative views and values, these videos have reached a certain type of person, namely Libertarian and Republican supporters of Ron and Rand Paul.

I think it is kind of humorous that I have become a spokesperson in my own way for Libertarian conservatism, since nothing in my background would seem to indicate that I would identify with the philosophical and political tenets of Libertarianism. Yet, over the years, I have become increasingly concerned with the national debt and the erosion of our civil liberties. With the help of some dedicated Ron Paul disciples, I have come full circle and now espouse a brand of small government political philosophy I now call, "Christian Libertarianism." In this brief article, I would like to explain to you my political philosophy and creed.

Christ-Centered and Conservative Evangelicalism

While I come from an extremely liberal and progressive family context, I have come to believe in an Evangelical Christian expression of historic Christianity. That is, I very much believe in and focus on Jesus Christ. I believe in the historic doctrine of the Trinity and that Jesus Christ is the Son of God, whom God the Father sent to die on the cross for our sins and rise again from the dead to give us eternal life. I also believe the Bible is the exclusively inspired and inerrant Word of God. I also believe the Bible is our only authority in matters of Christian faith and doctrine. "All scripture *is* given by inspiration of God, and *is* profitable for doctrine, for reproof, for correction, for instruction in righteousness" (2 Timothy 3:16).

I also believe that salvation is a free gift that God bestows upon His elect by grace alone. In fact, I believe we are justified by God's grace alone, through our faith alone in the person and redemptive work of Jesus Christ alone. I believe this based on the authority of God's Word alone and that all of life should done for the glory of God alone "And *whatever* you *do, in word or deed, do* everything in the name of the Lord" (Colossians 3:17).

Small Government, Pro-Life and Pro-Civil Liberties Conservatism

I have come to believe that the best government is the least amount of government. That is, I fundamentally believe the federal government is grown too big and is now out of control. I also believe that federal government spends tax generated money on far too many programs and initiatives that we can do without. I personally believe the $18 trillion dollar national debt is unsustainable and must be eradicated less America be reduced to insolvency. I believe in reducing the size and power of the federal government and eliminating unnecessary legislation and agencies of government such as the *Patriot Act*, NSA, TSA, and the IRS.

As a devout, Bible-believing Evangelical who wants to honor Jesus Christ with every aspect of my life, I believe that life begins at conception and I cannot support the Roe vs. Wade Supreme Court verdict of 1973. I strongly advocate the defense of life and want to be active in the pro-life movement.

As a conservative who very much cares about our civil liberties and rights as outlined by the U.S. Constitution, I very much believe that the government's policy of spying on our cell phone calls and the collection of this cell phone data is unconstitutional and should be abolished at once. As a person who believes in human autonomy and independence from authoritarian control, I want to reduce the size and reach of the federal government and get the government out our personal, private, fiscal and sexual lives.

A Call for Conservative Activism

As a loyal citizen of the United States of America, I want to be active to make the best version of America possible. I want to create a massive movement of citizen-patriots who care about the U.S. Constitution and who want make a difference in our generation. I want to advocate small government and pro-life and pro-civil liberties conservatism at the local, statewide and national levels. I want to make a difference in America for the Kingdom of God and Glory of Christ.

My creed is Jesus Christ and my mission is to transform America.

Donald Trump and Rand Paul Have Little in Common

A worldview is the way a person looks at the world. Technically speaking, a worldview is the fundamental cognitive orientation of an individual or society encompassing the entirety of the individual or society's knowledge and point of view. The Germans called one's worldview or comprehensive perspective on life a "Weltanschauung."

When you look at the different candidates running for the Republican nomination in 2016, it is clear that there could not be two fundamentally different worldviews than those articulated by Senator Rand Paul and Billionaire hotel developer and reality television personality Donald J. Trump. The radical differences in ideology and perspective between the two candidates are indicative of where American culture is at presently.

Rand Paul is a fundamentally a man of principle and of ideas. The essence of Rand Paul consists of what he believes and fights for. His small government and pro-civil liberties conservatism is the essence of his being. Rand Paul ran for and won his current U.S. Senate seat because of his ideas.

However, in stark contrast, Donald Trump's campaign is about himself. He released his first series of policy positions only *yesterday* because his campaign ultimately has never really been about "Making America Great Again," whatever that means, it has been all about the rich, famous and brash Donald J. Trump in all his glory.

Rand Paul's school newspaper columns at Baylor University in the early 1980's show a young man who was a small government and fiscal conservative from the beginning. On the other hand, Donald Trump's early and most recent career show that he has been all over the map both politically and ideologically.

In recent years Trump has been anything but a conservative politically, having supported abortion on demand, gun control, single payer health insurance, Obamacare and high taxes for the wealthy. While Rand Paul has been a life-long Republican, Trump only recently became some sort of a "Republican," having spent years as both a Democrat and an Independent. Sure, Trump has been making crazy policy statements of late, but the essence of Trump is Trump and not about concrete and substantive ideas and ideology.

Yet, it has never really been about what Donald Trump believes and stands for. It all reality, Trump's campaign is about Trump and his ideas don't really matter to most of his followers. Sadly, the Republican Party could very well nominate a man who has been anything but a faithful Republican.

Rand Paul is the Best America Has to Offer

Friends, there is no question that Rand Paul has the best ideas of any one of the Republican candidates running for President. Yet, because of his direct assault against entrenched Washington machine politics he is hated by the mainstream media and Republican establishment.

This means that we need to dig a little deeper for our candidate. We all can give a little more of our time and money to help Rand Paul win the election.

We all can volunteer our time and energies in creative and innovative ways to spread Senator Paul's unique small government and pro-civil liberties conservatism.

I remember observing an elderly lady at the mall a few years ago. Long since retired, this 75 plus grandmother set up a table at the mall and was handing out Bibles and invitations to her church. We all can set up tables in our neighborhood or local college campuses and talk to college students about why Senator Paul is a very different kind of candidate.

We all can dig deeper and give just a little bit more of ourselves.

The Quest for Liberty in the Selfie Generation

A few years ago I read about a plastic surgeon in Los Angeles who crashed his expensive sports car and died while driving and texting. It was revealed later that he had his prized pet poodle in his lap while he plummeted to his fiery death. Some witnesses said the plastic surgeon never looked up from his cell phone to notice the warning and detour signs indicating that construction workers were repairing a massive pothole that had developed over time on that part of the highway.

Welcome to the "selfie generation" where people would rather take digital self-portraits of themselves and text while driving or walking rather than pay attention to the real world. Our generation is one of rampant narcissistic indulgence and in reality, when we check our profile status all day, we worship ourselves…

In this culture of distraction there are very real issues facing American society and government. The United States of America now faces a national debt that is now over $18 trillion dollars and very few people seem to care that the federal government is spying on the very phones they check their Facebook status and send their incessant texts and selfies from.

This is the challenge of our times. It is hard to communicate to our friends, loved ones and neighbors that America is in deep political and fiscal trouble when all they care about is being perpetually entertained.

Republican and Libertarian Friends

Today I would like to launch a movement called, "Republicans and Libertarians United for Rand Paul." For too long America has gone down the path of big government and big spending.

The result has been an unmitigated disaster for the United States of America. Tax and spend big state liberalism has caused our $18 trillion dollar national debt, a crisis of massive proportions.

It is time for like-minded small government and pro-civil liberties Republicans and Libertarians to come together for a common cause.

In 2016, I would like to encourage my Republican and Libertarian friends to work together to see Rand Paul become the next President of the United States.

Also, a word for all the Independent voters out there! You are welcome to join us too. America is too great and our future to bright to be divided. Let us come together for the common good, let us come together for Rand Paul.

Please listen to this special podcast entitled, "Republicans and Libertarians United for Rand Paul" and take a stand for liberty and Rand Paul!

On the Trump / Kelly Feud

Fox News anchor Megyn Kelly is taking her second vacation since her confrontational performance at the Republican Primary debate in Cleveland, Ohio.

She assured her audience it had nothing to do with her spat with Donald Trump in the aftermath of the debate.

On her Wednesday broadcast, Kelly declared she would be taking a vacation, "starting immediately."

It is interesting that Kelly is taking such a long vacation in the wake of such a controversial week for her. Perhaps Fox News' Roger Ailes has something to do with that.

All we know is that Trump and Ailes has a kiss and make up session since the debate last Thursday Night and now Megyn Kelly is on her second vacation since the debate (you do the math).

Donald Trump is one powerful and snotty billionaire. Perhaps Ailes caved on Trump to avoid an all out war which would be bad for Fox's ratings. This is especially the case since last week's debate was viewed by 24 million dollars. It was a very lucrative night for Richard Murdoch, Roger Ailes and Fox News. Of course Fox is denying this is why Megyn Kelly is now sleeping with the fishes. Stay tuned folks. We will see if Megyn makes it back on the air.

Is Donald Trump the new Lex Luthor? If you are not familiar with the loquacious Lex, he is Superman's arch-nemesis in DC Comic lore. While there has been various story lines involving Lex Luthor, the one that I connect with the most is the one that depicts Lex as an evil billionaire corporate raider who turns to politics and through a nefarious turn of events, becomes President of the United States.

Lex Luthor, not unlike a scenario I foresee Donald Trump entering into, wins the election on a platform the stresses his business acumen. Luthor's first action as president in the DC comic version was to argue for a moratorium on fossil-based fuels.

I am not sure which is stranger, Superman's archenemy becoming President or the billionaire real estate and reality television personality Donald J. Trump running for President now.

However it turns out, one thing is certain, Donald Trump has turned the Republican Presidential primary race into a comic book.

Despite maintaining a commanding lead in most political polls, many Republicans are concerned about Donald Trump's actual views. Forever erratic, Donald Trump has been all over the place in his political affiliations and his positions on issues important to conservatives are shocking.

It is a well-documented fact that Donald Trump has been both a Democrat and Republican in recent years and has held very questionable views on taxes, healthcare, the right to life, gun control and a whole host of other issues facing conservatives.

The reality is, Donald Trump has a track record of supporting abortion rights and leftist political causes such as Obamacare, Universal Health Care, gun control, high taxes and abortion. Trump is down on record as being a big Hillary Clinton fan in the past, but now he is running as a "conservative" Republican.

How long will Donald Trump's hijacking of the Republican Party continue? If the GOP faithful does not wake up and smell what the celebrity apprentice has cooking, he may con his way all the way to winning the Republican nomination.

This would be tragic however, because for many of us who have been Republicans all our lives, there is reason to believe that Trump is engaged in the "art of the steal."

That is, this fake conservative, as Senator Rand Paul called him in a special campaign ad yesterday, is stealing the Republican nomination from authentic conservatives like Paul who have spent their lives in consistent defense of small-government conservatism.

The name of the game for Donald J. Trump is "the art of the steal."

Is Donald Trump really a Democratic operative working for Hillary Clinton? It may sound outrageous, but Trump could very well have been secretly planted by a cabal of Democrats and Hillary to confound and sow discord in the Republican Party.

While we are at it, why is Donald Trump in the Republican primaries in the first place? This is a guy who was a Democrat who believed in partial birth abortion and single payer health plans. I don't trust Donald Trump as far as I could throw him. I think Rand Paul was right today to question Trump's loyalty today. Please listen to my podcast tonight and find out why!

Bernie Sanders is Surging and Hillary Better Watch Out!

While many Americans are fixated upon the Donald Trump saga, many are unaware of the sensation that is being caused by far left U.S. Senator Bernie Sanders of Vermont. Bernard "Bernie" Sanders is the junior United States Senator from Vermont and a candidate for the Democratic Party's nomination for President in the 2016 U.S. presidential election.

According to the Los Angeles Times, Senator Bernie Sanders is presently drawing the largest crowds of any candidate running for President in either party Sanders drew a crowd his campaign estimated at 27,500 to the Los Angeles Memorial Sports Arena, including those in an overflow area outside, watching on giant video screens. Over the weekend, 28,000 people turned out to see him in Portland, Ore., and a campaign stop in Seattle pulled 15,000.

Hillary Clinton and establishment Democrats need to take note of Sanders. The self-professed progressive liberal is surging at an unbelievable rate and could very well win the nomination if Clinton is not careful.

A Sanders Nomination would be good news for many Republicans and could potentially be a repeat of 1972 when liberal Senator George McGovern lost to President Nixon is major drubbing. However, do not underestimate Mr. Sanders. The progressive base was a key factor in Barack Obama's ascendency to the U.S. Presidency. Could lighting strike twice for Mr. Sanders? Only time will tell.

Yet for now, he is a rock star to the far left and a socialist one at that.

The Deep Web of Lies that is Hillary and Bill Clinton

Breaking News, the BBC reports that Hillary Clinton has agreed to hand over to the FBI the private email server that she used as secretary of state. Her use of private email has generated a barrage of criticism as Mrs. Clinton runs for president.

According to the BBC, critics say that her set-up was unsecure, contrary to government policy and designed to shield her communications from oversight. The FBI is investigating whether classified information was improperly sent via the server and stored there. The BBC says that Mrs. Clinton initially handed over thousands of pages of emails to the state department, but not the server. Her lawyers will also hand over to the FBI memory sticks which contain the copies of the emails.

Her use of private email according to the BBC has been a major issue in the presidential race. Polls show an increasing number of voters view her as "untrustworthy" due in part to the questions surrounding her email use. Under US federal law, officials' correspondence is considered to be US government property.

This is not the first time the Clinton's have been caught in a web of lies. In fact, there is a pattern of lies and deception that go back decades. Do you recall the Monica Lewinsky and Gennifer Flowers scandals? How about the Paul Jones sexual misconduct scandal or Whitewater? Pick your poison and name your scandal, Bill and Hillary

Clinton have been masters at this for years. The Clinton's sit on a throne of lies and hopefully this email server will be Hillary's undoing.

Rand Paul Alone Can Win the Swing States

Forget Donald Trump, Jeb Bush as the other GOP pretenders, *only Rand Paul* can win Ohio, Iowa, Colorado, Virginia and the other key battleground swing states necessary to pick up the 270 electoral votes needed to win the Presidency in 2016.

While Rand Paul trails the likes of Donald Trump and Jeb Bush in recent Republican national polls overall, Trump and Bush trail Hillary Clinton badly in the above mentioned key swing states.

It is important to note that no Republican has ever been elected President without winning the battleground state of Ohio and out of the major Republican candidates, the polls show only Rand Paul can beat Clinton in Ohio.

It is crucial that Republicans pick a nominee that can actually win in November, 2016. All the evidence points that Donald Trump, Jeb Bush, Marco Rubio and the other Republican nominees losing badly to Hillary Clinton in a head to head match up in the general election in 2016.

However, Rand Paul holds a slight lead over Clinton in five key battleground states. This needs to be factored in when the primary season starts early next year.

Rand Paul supporters out there, please spread this around, only Rand can beat Hillary in 2016!

In Defense of the POW and MIA Movement in America

 Enough is enough my friends. Enough is enough! Have you grown weary of the militant political correctness and left-wing activism in this country? I most certainly have and have decided to fight back against the onslaught of liberal and progressive revisionism of American history and tradition. Today, I would like to call your attention to *Newsweek* Magazine online op/ed article entitled, "It's Time to Haul down another Flag of Racist Hate."

The article, written by liberal activist Rick Perlstein, a national correspondent of the *Washington Spectator*, vehemently argues that the POW/MIA flag is racist and spreads a "pernicious myth." Perlman says,

"You know that racist flag? The one that supposedly honors history but actually spreads a pernicious myth? And is useful only to venal right-wing politicians who wish to exploit hatred by calling it heritage? It's past time to pull it down."

Perlstein (B.A. University of Chicago), is a liberal Democrat, activist and author of *Before the Storm: Barry Goldwater and the Unmaking of the American Consensus* (2001), which won the 2001 Los Angeles Times Book Prize for history, and *Nixonland: The Rise of a President and the Fracturing of America (2008),* which was recognized as a notable book of the year by the New York Times.

Perlstein is also the author of *The Invisible Bridge* (2014) which has received a harsh critic by some pundits and scholars for its shoddy scholarship, improper citations and alleged plagiarism.

Rick Perlstein is no objective bystander to the liberal assault on American tradition and cherished values like honoring our veterans and POW /MIA's. It is a documented fact that Mr. Pelstein, until 2009, was a Senior Fellow at the far left "Campaign for America's Future," where he wrote for their blog against conservative politics called, *The Big Con*.

In Perlstein's *Newsweek* hatchet piece he also argues that Richard Nixon invented the cult of the "POW/MIA" in order to justify the carnage in Vietnam. Perlstein goes on to say in this so called "opinion" piece, that China manufactured stories of MIA in Vietnamese prison camps in order to keep the U.S. from normalizing relations with China's Asian rival Vietnam.

The Vietnamese prison camps were not a myth Mr. Perlstein, just ask Senator John McCain who spent over five years of his life in a dark and dirty cell as a prisoner of the North Vietnamese. In October 1967, McCain, while on a bombing mission over Hanoi was shot down, gravely injured and held capture as a prisoner of war by the Vietcong until 1973. McCain received lifelong injuries in "Hanoi Hilton," Mr. Pelstein and America's Prisoners of War and Missing in Action during the Vietnam War was not a myth.

Perlstein's opinion piece it's Time to haul down another Flag of Racist Hate" does a grave disservice to the almost 60,000 men and women who lost their lives in Vietnam. It also gravely besmirches the service and sacrifices of our

American military personal who suffered great losses in Vietnam.

And yes, Mr. Pelstein, many of them were prisoners of war and missing in action in that grave far eastern conflict and your article does nothing but undermine their honor and great courage. Following the Paris Peace Accords of 1973, 591 American prisoners of war (POW's) were returned during "Operation Homecoming." The United States has listed some 1,350 brave prisoners of war and approximately 1,200 American's who reported killed in action was and their bodies were never recovered. This Newsweek piece is not worthy of their memory.

It is time for those who love America to stand against the assaults of the politically-correct left who seek to rewrite and revise America's sacred history. The buck stops here Mr. Perlstein. I am one conservative and patriot who will speak out and stand up for the greatness of America.

Today I honor every single person who served in the Vietnam War. I am not worthy to defend you but I will and I must. Here I stand, so help me God. I can do nothing less.

 I just wanted to encourage you not to give up and fight for Rand Paul! I want to see a massive movement in support of Rand Paul build around the country. You know and I know that Rand has the best ideas of any candidate running for President. We just need to band together and fight for our man!

Here is a special message for all you Rand Paul supporters. Let's fight to the good fight for the best person running for President!

Rand Paul is Right to Decry the Patriot Act

If anyone was looking past Donald Trump and paying attention, there was a fierce exchange between Senator Rand Paul and NJ Governor Chris Christie last Thursday night's Republican Presidential debate on Fox News. The point of contention between the two famous Republican leaders has to do with provisions under the Patriot Act that allows for the federal government to search a person's person, property and effects without a warrant as long as the person being searched is suspected by the federal government of participating in "terrorist activities."

I for one was paying attention and believe Senator Paul was absolutely correct to deem any searches and seizures without a warrant an unconscionable breech of the 4th Amendment which clearly states;

"The right of the people to be secure in their persons, houses, papers, and effects, against unreasonable searches and seizures, shall not be violated, and no Warrants shall issue, but upon probable cause, supported by Oath or affirmation, and particularly describing the place to be searched, and the persons or things to be seized."

I, like Senator Paul, am particularly aghast at the Patriot Act's permission to give law enforcement officers permission to search a home of business without the owner's or the occupant's consent or knowledge. I am also troubled with the Patriot Act's the expanded use of national security letters, which allows the FBI to search telephone, e-mail, and financial records without a court order; and the expanded access of law enforcement agencies to business records, including library and financial records.

I concur with Senator Rand Paul that these extra-constitutional provisions are unconstitutional and I believe Paul should be commended by all Americans for standing up for our civil liberties and rights as clearly delineated by the U.S. Constitution.
One of the biggest problems with the Patriot Act is the definition of "Terrorism" and "Terrorists." While today members of Al-Qaeda and ISIS are deemed "terrorists," a future government could the provisions of the Patriot Act to deem any partisan group that is not in support of a given President's or governments polices as "terrorists."

Right now the Southern Poverty Law Center has deemed many conservative groups it opposes as "hate groups," who is to say that a future White House might now deem a conservative group a terrorist group under the Patriot Act? The recent scandal involving the IRS and its discrimination against conservative groups conclusively demonstrates that the Obama administration has targeted conservatives and has attempted to thwart their mobility and activities.

Who is to say that a future administration would not deem a dissenting person or group to be a terrorist threat under the Patriot Act? For these reasons alone, Senator Rand Paul should be applauded for his courageous stand against the Patriot Act, NSA and the buffoonery of Chris Christie.

On the 2nd Amendment

It is never right to assume something about a person based on surface level observations. People assume a lot of things about me because where I have lived and where I have went to school. Here on the East Coast, many people think I am a dumb hick because I lived and went to school in Texas and many of my friends back in Texas think I am liberal because I now go to school in an Ivy League town. Both of these assumptions are dead wrong.

I graduated at the top of my class and was an academic scholarship winning dean's list student in college, so the "dumb hick" stigma simply does not apply to me. Also, I am most certainly not a "liberal" since there is very little about me and my beliefs that could be classified in the progressive or liberal political or ideological camp.

I think the time has come for me to be clear about something that I hold dear to myself. I strongly support gun ownership and the right to keep and bear arms. Not only that, I believe in what is called, "open carry." That is, I believe that every law abiding adult citizen of the United States, who is not a felon, should be able to lawfully keep a firearm on their person.

I have spoken to a lot of gun control advocates since I have been on the East Coast and have heard their arguments against lawful gun ownership and they are entirely unconvincing to me. I simply want to have what the U.S. Constitution permits me to have, nothing more and nothing less.

Mike Huckabee or Ben Carson for President?

Over the last few months many of my Evangelical friends have expressed to me that they have decided to vote for Mike Huckabee or Ben Carson for President and some have tried to get me on board with these two fine Christian gentlemen as well. These friends of mine believe the time has come for a truly Christian leader to emerge upon the scene to return America "back to its Christian roots." These faith-based voters want to see prayer returned back into public schools, gay marriage ended, abortion abolished and Jesus Christ as Lord of all.

Now, I understand their concerns, I really do. In fact, I come from a devout Evangelical Christian background and graduated from the same Southern Baptist School that Mike Huckabee attended back in the day. I also went to several other Evangelical schools and some of the most prominent Evangelical Churches in America. So, I know the Evangelical culture and concerns very, very well. In fact, I would still consider myself an Evangelical Christian. However, I am not the kind of Evangelical that frowns upon dancing, playing cards, going to the movies or other "worldly entertainments."

Historically, among many other things, Evangelicals have believed in the authority and inspiration of the Bible alone, the centrality of the Gospel of Jesus Christ and the need to be a "witness for Christ" in our secular culture. Now, I am in full agreement with all those sentiments. Yet, I simply do not believe that being a strong Evangelical Christian necessarily translates to being a good political candidate. In fact, George W. Bush was one of the most vocal and alleged "Evangelicals" ever in the history of America. Yet, W's policies were among the all-time worst in American political history.

In fact, I believe a person could be the best Christian imaginable but a bad Presidential candidate. In the case of Mike Huckabee, he was anything but a small government conservative while governor of Arkansas and his record shows that he raised taxes and was very much into "big government."

The Cato Institute says the following about Mike Huckabee:

"As governor of Arkansas, Huckabee dramatically increased state spending. During his two-term tenure, spending increased by more than 65 percent — at three times the rate of inflation.

The number of government workers increased by 20 percent, and the state's debt services increased by nearly $1 billion. Huckabee financed his spending binge with higher taxes. Under his leadership, the average Arkansan's tax burden increased 47 percent, according to the Arkansas Democrat-Gazette, including increases in the state's gas, sales, income, and cigarette taxes. He raised taxes on everything from groceries to nursing home beds.

Huckabee answers these complaints by pointing out that he "cut taxes 94 times" while governor. True. But most of those tax cuts were tiny, like exempting residential lawn care from the sales tax. Some cuts reduced overall state revenues by as little as $15,000. On net, Huckabee increased state taxes by more than $500 million. In fact,

Huckabee increased taxes in the state by more than Bill Clinton did."

Please see: http://www.cato.org/publications/commentary/huckabee-biggest-biggovernment-conservative

Again, don't get me wrong, I personally like Mike Huckabee. I really do. I understand Mike Huckabee and his voting demographic more than you will ever know. I respect Mike's faith in Jesus Christ. I believe in Jesus as well, I am just not sure that in the case of Mike Huckabee that one's Christian faith and commitment is the sole criteria we should base our political decisions on.

The same goes with Ben Carson. I love the guy. I have no complaints against Ben Carson's Christian character. The man is a saint and I would be the first person in line if Ben Carson was speaking on his work as a doctor at a Christian breakfast down at the First Baptist Church of Dallas. I just see very little actual political experience on Ben Carson's vast resume.

The reality is, almost all the candidates running for President in the GOP are professing Christians. While we are at it, Rand Paul has devoted his spare time to do medical missions trips and both Scott Walker and Ted Cruz's dads were Christian ministers. Heck, Jimmy Carter claims to be Baptist and Donald Trump a good Presbyterian, does that mean I should vote for either one of these guys?

So, in attempting to differentiate all these great Christians from each other, I think we need to look into their policies and records on the issues and not what they taught in Sunday school this past weekend. Because of my Evangelical background, you will not see any personal attacks on Ben Carson and Mike Huckabee from me, yet I am not voting for these guys because I have learned from experience that being a Jesus freak does not always translate into good politics.

On the Bizarre, Strange Trip that has Become American Politics

 "Be careful about fighting monsters, lest you become a monster too. For when you gaze too long into the abyss, the abyss looks back at you" (Friedrich Nietzsche).

During the Clinton administration, I thought America had reached an all-time low when it was exposed that the most powerful leader in the world had a sordid affair with a young intern named Monica Lewinsky. But to Bill Clinton's credit, he was able to multi-task and run the country all the while getting his groove on.

Besides, despite his titanic lapses of moral judgement, Bill Clinton was educated at Georgetown, Yale and Oxford and was a highly skilled and qualified politician who navigated the greatest era of prosperity in post-WW2 society. Despite the hubris of this own personal scandal, America was still stable and functioned as it had in previous generations.

Yet, there is something unfathomable and intensely surreal transpiring before our very eyes. The whole political discourse of this country has plummeted into the gutter and has been car jacked by a reality TV show personality with a bad comb over. The storied land of Washington, Lincoln and Reagan has been overrun by the Jerry Springer Show.

Yet, there is a truth to the old colloquial adage; "garbage in, garbage out." That is, if one focuses on what is bad and sordid in society, he or she runs the risk of taking on those same detrimental characteristics. America has reached an all-time low in allowing a loud mouthed billionaire and hubris driven reality show personality take over the political narrative of the most powerful nation in the world because much of America is fixated on pop culture and its troubled personalities.

America has always loved its pop culture celebrities but in times past we would have never conceived of having Elvis or Frank Sinatra becoming President of the United States. Yet, entertainment has now become reality in the United States as the great American train wreck that is Donald Trump has captivated the nation as 24 million Americans watched Fox News' Republican Debate with suspense filled fascination. Like those gawkers who cause traffic jam on the freeway because they just cannot look away from a bad car wreck, America just cannot look away from the debacle and spectacle that is the one and only Donald Trump.

I am convinced that the same elements in American society who love the Jerry Springer show or the talentless Kim Kardashian are the ones driving the great American political train wreck that is the Donald Trump Show. Kim Kardashian's only claim to fame is that she produced a bootleg pornographic video that was released on the internet. In the same vein, many people are fascinated with

Donald Trump's freak show because the billionaire real estate and media tycoon is political porn. People know they should look away from his vulgar tirades but they just can't.

The tragedy of American politics today is that instead of focusing on important issues like reducing America's unsustainable $18 trillion dollar debt or concentrating on Obama's unwise nuclear deal with Iran, we are spending all our time looking in on the great American train wreck that is Donald Trump. We all know his epic meltdown and implosion lurks right around the corner and we just can't look away.

How a Trump Republican Nomination Could Doom America

Now that the first Republican debate of the 2016 primary season has come and gone, one thing is certain, Mr. Donald Trump is going nowhere. The reality is, Republicans across America need to start getting worried about Donald Trump's chances of winning the nomination next summer. Sure, a lot could happen, but this life-long Republican smells trouble in the air at night.

Donald Trump could do one of three things in the coming election cycle. The first scenario has Trump bowing out gracefully and watching the election from the sidelines (highly unlikely). The second scenario has Donald Trump actually winning the nomination and badly losing in the general election to Ms. Hillary Rodham Clinton. The last scenario, which is just as nefarious for Republicans, is that Donald Trump could go Ross Perot on us and run as a third party candidate. That would cause major headaches for us Republicans because a split vote would most likely tip the election to Clinton and that would have devastating consequences for the United States of America.

Mr. Trump is the wild card and he knows it. After decades of being a very rich hotel and media mogul, Mr. Apprentice wants to be at center stage. To me, this appears to be a big game to Mr. Trump. He loves the spotlight and all the world is his stage. However, many pundits and astute observers of American history believe this coming election in 2016 will be the definitive election in a generation. The stakes are high and many disaffected Republicans are betting on loose cannon with the future of America on the line. As the tragic and historic Supreme Court verdicts of this summer demonstrate, who we choose for President could affect generations of Americans.

While the President of the United States is most certainly not our king, he or she wields enormous political and real power in this country. The President selects Supreme Court Justices who almost always get nominated by our hapless Congress. The President of the United States is the most powerful person on earth and many Republicans are throwing the dice when they lend their support to Donald Trump.

A trump nomination will most certainly win the White House for Bill and Hillary Clinton. This will be tragic because America is too great of a country to be destroyed by liberalism. It is time for the Republican faithful to bounce Trump and kick this loudmouth to the curb.

On Rand Paul, Republican Debates and Chris Christie

I am sure glad that Libertarian Republican Rand Paul stood up against RINO Republican Chris Christie and defended the 4th Amendment.

Chris Christie is the horrible governor of New Jersey, the state with the highest taxes in the United States. Here are my thoughts on Rand Paul's smack down on Chris Christie whom Rand handled like a boss.

A special edition of "The Lee Enochs Show" (America's Most Controversial Podcast)

I never believed in conspiracy theories until watching the Fox News Republican debate last night. I thought something was off when Fox and the other media agencies did not let Rand's father speak very much during the 2008 and 2012 Republican presidential debates, but I had no hard evidence of a conspiracy.

However, something is definitely amiss in the Republican Party and Fox News. There is no question that Rand Paul was not given his fair share of air time to express his views. In fact he was dead last in total time on air (roughly five minutes) to Donald Trump's air time (over eleven minutes).

This is unfortunate because Rand Paul clearly won the debate. Sure, Donald Trump did not implode like many of were hoping, but if anyone was actually watching the Fox News debate, that would have seen Rand Paul absolutely decimate centrist RINO Chris Christie on live cable television. Christie's arguments supporting unlawful searches and seizures was pitiful and Rand Paul won that exchange hands down. As a student of the U.S. Constitution, Paul's arguments were squarely rooted in the 4th Amendment which states clearly,

The right of the people to be secure in their persons, houses, papers, and effects, against unreasonable searches and seizures, shall not be violated, and no warrants shall issue, but upon probable cause, supported by oath or affirmation, and particularly describing the place to be searched, and the persons or things to be seized.

Fox News seems to think that Rand Paul has no chance in winning the nomination next year and so gave him the least amount of time. This is shameful because Fox needs to stop playing kingmaker and just report the news. Fox News does not make "the news." It is not the "news." It is merely a servant of the people and needs to stop interjecting itself into these Republican debates as though this news agency alone dictates who will be the Republican nominee in 2016.

I think it was a good debate overall. However, Donald Trump, while high on spunk, was short on substance. Also, Jeb Bush proved again that he just not ready to be a prime time player at this level.

Rand Paul deserves equal air time in these debates. Pass this on to your Republican friends. He was stellar in this debate and utterly manhandled Chris Christie on the 4th Amendment. For this reason alone last night's Fox News Republican debate was a joy to watch. Rand Paul won overall and it's just too bad he was not given more air time.

The big event many of us Republicans have wanted has finally arrived. Tonight at the house Lebron James built known as Quicken Loans arena in Cleveland, Ohio, Fox News will commence the first Republican presidential primary debate for the 2016 election.

It should be interesting as real estate tycoon and GOP front runner Donald Trump will take center stage in tonight's event and finally be confronted and engaged by his fellow Republican candidates. Conventional wisdom leads me to believe that Trump will be his normal blowhard and bombastic self, fair poorly in the debate but will survive and live another day to offend another large voting demographic. But who knows? Trump's whole campaign could implode before our very eyes tonight as his ego cannot resist saying outrageous things to draw attention to himself.

This also could be the beginning of the end for Jeb Bush, the scion of Republican royalty that seems to make a major verbal gaffe every other day on the campaign trail. This could be the night when Jeb Bush crumples like the paper dragon many of know he really is. Let's face it folks, Jeb Bush has been humiliating himself and his family dynasty with his ill-timed comments such as saying that "a half a billion dollars is too much to spend on women's health issues."

Tonight also could be a big night for Republican leaders such as Rand Paul, Ted Cruz, Scott Walker and Ben Carson as they each try to break free from the pack and emerge at the top of the heap. Marco Rubio and Mike Huckabee will try to do the same.

The two people that could potentially surprise a lot of people tonight are Texas Senator Ted Cruz and former Arkansas Governor Mike Huckabee. Many people are unaware of how good a public speaker Huckabee is and he clearly did himself a great favor by his great debate performances during the 2008 Republican primary season. Ted Cruz on the other hand, is another story.

Many people forget or are entirely oblivious to the fact that Cruz was a legendary national debate champion at Princeton during his undergraduate years and clearly demonstrated his intellectual acumen by excelling at Harvard Law School and as the Solicitor General of Texas. While serving as the top attorney of the Lone Star state, Cruz successfully argued several cases before the U.S. Supreme Court. All this to say, that if Ted Cruz is actually allowed to debate tonight, he could emerge victorious.

Another person who could shine tonight if given a chance is Kentucky Senator Rand Paul, the son of Ron, the legendary Libertarian hero. Rand Paul, in my estimation has clearly the best ideas of all the candidates running for the Republican Presidential nomination. If Paul is actually allowed to articulate himself tonight and is not cut off and muzzled like his father was constantly in the 2008 and 2012 Republican contests, he could make a definite splash with his small government and civil liberties perspective.

What we need to see tonight is confident candidates who can clearly articulate why they should be elected President of the United States of America.

We also need to see all the candidates address the reality of the corrosive power of money in this election cycle wherein a wealthy oligarchy of donors is dominating the 2016 election in both the Republican and Democratic parties.

We also need to see each of the candidates discuss how they would attempt to tackle the $ 18 trillion dollar national debt and help turn America back into the powerful economic engine it had been for over a century.

Tonight the candidates also need to address the issue of our civil liberties and if they would cease the current Patriot Act policy of spying on innocent American's cell phone calls.

Rand Paul could distinguish himself as the candidate to beat if he is allowed to share his distinctive vision for balancing the federal budget, eradicating the national debt and preserving our privacy and cherished civil liberties.

Will this be the night that Donald Trump and Jeb Bush crumble badly under the media's red hot scrutiny? Or will a less publicized candidate emerge from the pack to become the favorite? All these questions and more could be answered tonight during the first Republican debate of the 2016 primary season.

Thoughts Before the Fox News Debate

Are you ready to rumble? As a life-long Republican and political junkie, I am very excited about the Fox News Republican debate coming up this Thursday. It should be interesting to say the least. Fox News has announced that ten Republican candidates will be participating in the debate that will be broadcasted live from Quicken Loans Arena in Cleveland, Ohio.

The ten that made the cut are real estate and reality TV mogul Donald Trump; former Florida Gov. Jeb Bush; Wisconsin Gov. Scott Walker; former Arkansas Gov. Mike Huckabee; retired neurosurgeon Ben Carson; Texas Sen. Ted Cruz; Florida Sen. Marco Rubio; Kentucky Sen. Rand Paul; New Jersey Gov. Chris Christie; and Ohio Gov. John Kasich.

This means that Rick Perry, Rick Santorum, Bobby Jindal, Lindsey Graham, George Pataki, Jim Gilmore and potential breakout star Carly Fiorina did not make the cut and will appear in the 5:00 pm undercard.

It is a tragic fall from grace for former three-time Texas Governor Rick Perry, the gaffe prone governor of one of America's most populous and prosperous states. This is unfortunate because the Lone Star state is experiencing an economic boon that needs to be celebrated and like him or not, Rick Perry has a lot to do with that.

After reviewing the main event scorecard, I am left wondering how Carly Fiorina was left off the list and centrist Chris Christie was made the cut. I know that Fox's decision to include or exclude a candidate was based on results from several polls. However folks, let's face it, there is no way in hades Chris Christie is going to be the Republican nominee in 2016 and Carly Fiorina could potentially be the VP pick come nominating time next Summer.

In looking at the ready for prime time debaters, I am left wondering if this will be reduced to being a Donald Trump ratings spectacle or if they will actually let each candidate have equal time. I am also left wondering, based on past experiences with these sorts of debates, if Rand Paul will actually be allowed to have equal time.

If you recall the 2008 and 2012 Republican Primary debates, the major networks most certainly did not allow Rand's father, Ron Paul have much air time. In fact, it was almost humorous how Fox News and the other networks cut away from Ron Paul to Mitt Romney.

A word to Fox News; Let Rand Paul speak!

Rand Paul has innovative and bold ideas that set him apart from the rest of the Republican candidates. Rand Paul's views concerning reducing the national debt, ending the Patriot Act and the NSA's spying on the American people's cell phone calls are important issues that need prime time emphasis this Thursday night. Sadly, Fox News will probably silence Rand like they did his father, time after time again.

If Fox News does not let Rand Paul speak and muzzle him like they did his father, this debate will be a tragedy we should call, "Silence of the Rand."

Why Rand Paul Won the C-SPAN Forum

As a graduate student in one of the greatest academic settings in the world, I have been trained to formulate good and cogent arguments that support my thesis. In fact, if I don't my professors will most certainly call me on any unsubstantiated claims in my papers. Case in point, last fall, while in my Political Philosophy course here in Princeton, I wrote what I thought was a rather clever paper on property rights and John Locke. I was wrong. It was not clever and my professor, one of the world's leading scholars on political philosophy called me on it. I think I recall his comments indicating that while he thought my paper was "innovative," I was "most certainly wrong" in my thesis.

Needless to say, words have meaning and ideas have consequences. In last night's C-SPAN Republican Presidential forum at St. Anselm College in Manchester, N.H. we saw the weakness of many of the candidates looking anything but "presidential." In fact, some of the candidates looked rather sheepish and withered badly under the glaring spotlight. Case in point, Jeb Bush, in attempting to distinguish himself from his brother and father, failed badly. Jeb Bush is just not a ready for prime time player and his comments were rather "bush league" for a man who has risen over $100 million dollars for his campaign thus far and is trying to prove he deserves to be the front runner. John McCain's BFF, Senator Lindsey Graham failed in his attempt to prove that he is anything but a third rate cheap suit and centrist hack.

As a person who traffics in the world of substantial ideas, I believe Senator Rand Paul won the battle of ideas and ultimately the entire C-SPAN forum by clearly differentiating himself from the same old Republican drivel. While pressed for time in such a bloated forum, Paul clearly showed himself to be a different kind of Republican that actually cares about civil liberties and due process. While it is very early in this Republican dog and pony show, I believe Rand Paul is the candidate with the best small government ideas going forward.

As I reflect upon this odd forum where so many candidates competed for such little time to formulate their ideas, some glaring things seem apparent. First of all, it is clear that Jeb Bush is not ready to be President of the local rotary club let alone leader of the free world. His performance was horrible for such a popular Republican candidate, proving that name recognition and buckets of money aren't anything if you can't articulate your vision. Marco Rubio also disappointed me and sounded like a George W. Bush war hawk. I believe Ted Cruz did a good job as did Scott Walker and Ben Carson. Bobby Jindal did better than expected and I was pleasantly surprised. Besides Rand Paul's victory of ideas, I believe the person who clearly distinguished herself was Carly Fiorina who showed she really has game.

One of the glaring issues for me pertains to Donald Trump. Where was the guy? How can the front runner not be at all these events? At some point Trump needs to show America that he can hang with the big boys and girls of the Republican Party. Also, where was Mike Huckabee, the darling of social conservatives? He did not help his cause by not showing up to this important venue. Rick Perry and Lindsey Graham should not have bothered to show up at all and failed miserably. Chris Christie and the rest of the GOP supporting cast have no chance at the nomination, so why bother? Rand Paul won the C-SPAN forum on ideas alone.

Problems with the Liberal Gospel

How should Christianity relate to the social order around them? How should Christians deal with poverty in technologically advanced Western Civilization? Does the Kingdom of God only affect a person individually or should it affect the entire social order of a given society?

These questions and others related to the possibility of formulating a Christian sociology in modern industrialized society are raised in Walter Rauschenbusch's book entitled, A Theology for the Social Gospel. Walter Rauschenbusch (1861-1918), was an influential American Baptist Pastor of German descent, who taught at Rochester Theological Seminary in upstate New York and is considered by many to be ideological father of the "Social Gospel" movement made popular by civil rights leaders Martin Luther King (1929-1968), Caesar Chavez (1927-1993) and other activists during the turbulent 20th Century. Rauschenbusch was greatly impacted by the grinding poverty and injustices he saw in the lives of his parishioners while serving as a pastor in New York Cities "Hell's Kitchen" neighborhood and attempted to formulate a distinctly Christian theology, sociology, and ministerial methodology that directly related to helping the urban poor and down trodden of a given society[1].

Summary

In A Theology for the Social Gospel, Rauschenbusch states that true and authentic Christianity opposes organized evil that represses and subjugates people and proposes that the "kingdom of God" establishes a just and equitable social life for all people (39). Rauschenbusch argues under the heading "The Challenge of the Social Gospel to Theology" (1-10), that we need to abandon undue dogmas and traditions and adapt the message of Christianity to the respective social-political setting it finds itself in. It must contextualize itself and make itself relevant to contemporary culture or run the risk of being eviscerated or rendered ineffectual by modern men and women. Rauschenbusch argues, "If theology stops growing or is unable to adjust itself to its modern environment and meet its present tasks, it will die (1).

Rauschenbusch postulates the thesis that Christianity must "establish some connection between religion and social feelings and experience" in order to reach many working and educated people within contemporary society who are "craving a social interpretation and application of Christianity" (3). Rauschenbusch argues that Protestant theology needs periodical reform and rejuvenation and as the Church stood for the essential Trinitarian doctrines of the Council of Nicaea and Luther's stand for the doctrine of Justification by grace through faith alone, the church should proceed with these reforming tendencies and adopt the social gospel as an essential tenet of the historic Christian faith (12-22).

In the second chapter of A Theology for the Social Gospel (9-22), Rauschenbusch argues for the "theological readjustment" of Christianity along "social gospel" lines. Rauschenbusch states, "The social gospel calls for an expansion in the scope of salvation and for more religious dynamic to the work of God" (11). Rauschenbusch furthermore argues for the abandonment of overtly doctrinal Christianity for a practical faith with an emphasis on the "kingdom of God" and the "simple arguments of Jesus" (16).

Rauschenbusch argues that the social gospel is the religion of the people and approximates the religious yearnings of all peoples irrespective of their backgrounds and is devoid of the excess doctrinal baggage that many Christians have been bogged down in (17).

Throughout A Theology for the Social Gospel, Rauschenbusch argues for a theology of the Kingdom of God, based on the simplicity of Jesus teachings found in the first three gospels. Rauschenbusch argues that Jesus came to preach a message of hope utilizing certain social and ethical teachings that liberate humanity from repression and genuinely lifts a person up from their harsh circumstances.

Rauschenbusch places a tremendous emphasis on his understanding of the "Kingdom of God" that had been long forgotten due to the undue Hellenization of Christianity (25). Rauschenbusch argues "the doctrine of the kingdom of God was left underdeveloped by individualistic theology and finally mislaid by it almost completely" (25).

Rauschenbusch argues in chapter three that such a social gospel view of the kingdom of God is neither alien nor novel to authentic Christianity but is ultimately what Jesus had in mind in his public ministry as detailed in the synoptic gospels. Rauschenbusch ultimately argues in his book that Christianity has been weighed down unduly by too much emphasis on propositional doctrine and must return to the practical and social teachings of Jesus that help a person in his or her particular economic and political context.

Rauschenbusch argues that Western Christianity has been overly influenced by the "competitive selfishness" of capitalism (29) and must return to a socialist model of economics. This socialist and anti-Capitalism view of economics is seen throughout the book . Rauschenbusch argues the social gospel liberates and sets a person free from the "consciousness of sin" (31-37) when a person realizes their place in the kingdom of God. Rauschenbusch also argues that the "social gospel opens our eyes" to the ways in which religious men are to implement the teachings of Jesus on earth (39).

Rauschenbusch summarizes the significance and importance of the social Gospel when he writes, "The social gospel is above everything practical. It needs religious ideas which will release energy for heroic opposition against organized evil and the building of a righteous social life" (42). In chapters four through ten (31-77), Rauschenbusch gives a liberal theological and social gospel understanding of the consciousness of sin, the fall of man, the nature and transmission of sin, the super-personal forces and the kingdom of evil and argues that the social gospel can help liberate people who have been repressed by sinful governments that have been corrupted through sin and the fall. Rauschenbusch further discusses the implications of the social gospel and Christian doctrine under chapters entitled, "The Social Gospel and Personal Salvation" (95-109), "The Salvation of the Supernatural Forces" (110-117), "The Church as the Social Factor of Salvation" (118-131), "The Kingdom of God" (131-145), "The Social Gospel and the Conception of God" (167-187), "The Holy Spirit, Revelation, Inspiration and Prophecy" (188-196), Baptism and the Lord's Supper: (197-207), "Eschatology" (208-239) and "The Social Gospel and the Atonement" (240-272).

Critical Evaluation

Throughout A Theology of the Social Gospel Rauschenbusch is guilty of the logical fallacies of Equivocation and Redefinition wherein the person postulating a given argument jettisons the normative linguistic and historical-grammatical usage of a term in order to attribute and utilize a fabricated meaning to a term without warrant or justification.

After manufacturing this spurious meaning of a given term, the person employing this less than honest rhetorical device then utilizes this spurious definition in attempting to further their argument. In other words, analogous to the false Biblical hermeneutical practice of Eisegesis (reading a false meaning into a text), a person arguing via Equivocation and Redefinition redefines a word or term and then runs with this false meaning of a word or term to make a point. In a Theology of the Social Gospel,

Rauschenbusch constantly redefines historic Christian theological terms along liberal theological Social Gospel lines and thus abandons the normative historic Christian doctrines pertaining to God, Sin and Salvation.

Rauschenbusch sees everything through the lens or paradigm or presupposition grid of the liberal Social Gospel and does not attribute the normative historic Christian meanings to important theological terms. Another logical fallacy Rauschenbusch utilizes throughout A Theology of the Social Gospel is the Red Herring fallacy of the use of a "Straw Man Argument" wherein one of the participants of a debate attributes a false position to his debate opponent and in turn attacks the false position instead of the actual argument made by his or her opponent. Logician T. Edward Damer writes, "The Straw Man is a type of Red Herring because the arguer is attempting to refute his opponent's position, and in the context is required to do so, but instead attacks a position—the "straw man"—not held by his opponent."[2]

Rauschenbusch is furthermore guilty of using a "Straw Man" line of argumentation against historic Christianity since he attributes to historic Christianity theological positions and arguments that historic Christianity in fact does not hold such For example, in the first chapter of A Theology of the Social Gospel, Rauschenbusch writes, "The social gospel is the old message of salvation, but large and intensified. The individualistic Gospel has taught us to see the sinfulness of every human heart and has inspired us with faith in the willingness and power of God to save every soul that comes to him.

But it has not given us an adequate understanding of the sinfulness of the social order and its share of sins of all individuals within it. It has not evoked faith in the will and power of God to redeem the permanent institutions of human society from their guilt and oppression and extortion" (5).

This just a blatantly false statement with no resemblance to the truth pertaining to historic Christianity which in the teachings of the Old Testament Prophets, Jesus Christ and the Apostles clearly deal with issue of societal equity and fairness irrespective of one's social and economic background. The Bible is replete with verses on social justice (See: Exodus 22:22, 23:6-11, Leviticus 19:15, Proverbs 22:16, 22:22, and 29:7). While it may be true that at the time Rauschenbusch wrote A Theology of the Social Gospel, that many Christians neglected the poor and repressed in society, there were also Christian ministries such as the Salvation Army that had been doing tremendous work among the needy in society long before Rauschenbusch emerged upon the scene to proclaim his "Social Gospel" that has more in common with Marxist and Socialist political ideology than it does authentic and historic Biblical Christianity.

A second deadly flaw of Rauschenbusch's A Theology of the Social Gospel is his reliance on liberal Protestant Theology in the guidance of his doctrinal views about God, humanity and the human condition. The "Kingdom of God" mentioned by Rauschenbusch is not one and the same thing with the Kingdom of God mentioned by Jesus Christ in the New Testament. Rauschenbusch's "Social Gospel" is not really the "Gospel of Jesus Christ" at all and the "Jesus Christ" mentioned in this book does not have a one to one connection with the true Jesus Christ of human history and the historic Christian faith. Rauschenbusch has recreated and redefined who Jesus Christ is in accordance with his Socialism and views on the Social Gospel.

For example, Rauschenbusch argues for the inherent veracity of his "Social Gospel" that functions autonomously outside the Christian Church when he says, "The Social Gospel does not need the aid of Church authority to get a hold of our hearts. It gets a hold in spite of such authority when necessary" (13). Rauschenbusch furthermore states that the Social Gospel will do for the Christian Church as what the theological findings of the Council of Nicaea and the Protestant Reformation (13). Hence, Rauschenbusch attributes massive, unprecedented and unparalleled importance to his version of the Social Gospel without historical warrant and Biblical justification.

Rauschenbusch is correct in h arguing that Christians need to be concerned about evil, poverty and repression in a given society, since this the command of Jesus in the Sermon of the Mount (Matthew 5-7) and elsewhere in the Bible, but his doctrinal views are not Biblical and in accordance with the authentic Christian Church he attempted to Reform along Social Gospel lines of thinking. In fact, I am not sure if Rauschenbusch was part of the true Christian Church at all.

Rauschenbusch greatly undermines the authority of the Holy Scriptures and the Apostles of our Lord Jesus Christ when he argues the following concerning the Apostle Paul, The great religious thinkers who created theology were always leaders who were shaping ideas to meet actual situations. The new theology of Paul was a product of fresh religious experience and of practical necessities. His idea that the Jewish law had been abrogated by Christ's death was worked out in order to set his mission to the gentiles free from the crippling grip of the past and to make an international religion of Christianity.

This above statement made by Rauschenbusch in A Theology of the Social Gospel is simply false and even heretical since it says that Paul's theology was formulated due to pragmatic issues instead of being via inspired revelation. Instead of Paul's theology being part of the exclusively authoritative, inspired, inerrant and infallible Word of God, Rauschenbusch rather argues that Pauline's theology was man made for a given situation.

Conclusion

Rauschenbusch's theological liberalism and political socialism is ultimately guiding his views of Christianity and when historic Christian teaching gets in the way of his liberal social gospel, it renders it meaningless and relegates all Christian doctrine that disagrees with his thesis to the ash heap of cultural irrelevancy. In A Theology of the Social Gospel, Rauschenbusch sacrifices the historic doctrines of the Christian faith on the nefarious twin altars of theological and political pragmatism and redefines Christianity for his own purposes.

Rauschenbusch is accurate in exhorting us to be concerned about the Kingdom of God, the present social order of things, the poor and the exploited among us, but it can be safely argued from an Evangelical and Bible believing perspective that Rauschenbusch's views concerning Christianity and the teachings of Christ, the Apostles and the Historic Christian Church are not one in the same by any stretch of the imagination.

In fact, the chasm fixed between historic Christianity and the liberal and pragmatic revisionism of Walter Rauschenbusch in A Theology of the Social Gospel is as wide as the gulf of infinitude fixed between rich man and Lazarus mentioned by our Lord in the Gospel of Luke Chapter 16.

On Cecil the Lion

"Therefore God also gave them up to uncleanness, in the lusts of their hearts, to dishonor their bodies among themselves, who exchanged the truth of God for the lie, and worshiped and served the creature rather than the Creator, who is blessed forever. Amen" (Romans 1:24-25).

As the global outrage over the killing of Cecil the Lion is being discussed around the world, I want to point out the irony of the fact that many of the most adamant supporters of animal rights conservation are the most militant advocates of abortion rights in Western culture.

While the death of the this beast of burden is tragic, what is more tragic is that close to 60 million babies in the United States have died via abortion since the Supreme Court's Historic Roe vs. Wade ruling in 1973.

Don't get me wrong; while I am a very big supporter of animal conservation, I believe it is a grotesque tragedy of massive proportions that many people in the West care more about a wild animal than a human being that is created in very image of God.

Western culture has plummeted into a narcissist culture of death where we worship animals and favor the destruction of human beings. This is the twisted and dark reality of the world we live in today.

From the horrific Planned Parenthood scandal to the everyday tragedy of abortion on demand throughout Western society, we have long since abandoned the notion that every single person matters.

I personally believe that the lives of the unborn matter. I personally stand with the historic Christian Church which teaches that human beings are created in the image of God and are endowed by their creator with certain inalienable rights such as life, liberty and the pursuit of happiness.

Our world has gone absolutely bad crazy insane. We now care about a wild animal more than a human being. We have lost our collective moorings and our Judeo-Christian values on the sanctity of human life. God have mercy on us all. We must choose life that we might live.

"Aye, fight and you may die. Run and you'll live — at least a while. And dying in your beds many years from now, would you be willing to trade all the days from this day to that for one chance, just one chance to come back here and tell our enemies that they may take our lives, but they'll never take our freedom!"

Many people have asked me why I have been making so many videos and taking so many very public stands lately.

Over the last several months it has dawned on me how short life really is. I realize that I may not have as much time as I thought. Life is quick and sooner than we think, it is over.

With the brevity of life in mind, I have decided to launch a full court press for freedom from government control.

You see my whole life I have tried to be a good Republican boy and do the right thing. I tried to conform to the spineless culture in which we live. I have tried to keep my mouth shut and just do what I am told. I have tried to conform to the upper middle class suburban culture that permeates the modern Republican Party.

I have tried to be a country club RHINO Republican and it just did not work for me. Like a fire burning within me, I have awakened to the realization that America the beautiful is under siege and that unless citizen patriots like you and me rise up and make a difference, then life as we know it in the United States is over.

Instead of living a life of conformity in mundane and controversy-free suburbia, I have decided to try to make a radical difference in America right here and right now.

Every day the federal government takes more and more of our personal liberties and freedoms away. Every day we are told by the left that we must conform to political correctness or run the risk of being exiled from polite society. I do not care anymore. America is too great and the promise of better days too inspiring for me to remain silent anymore.

It is time to live free or die hard. For they might take our lives, but they'll never take our freedom!

Why I am a Christian

By now, you probably know that I am a Christian. Yes, the rumors are true. I believe In Jesus Christ and my Christian faith is absolutely crucial to me. I believe in the historic doctrine of the Trinity that argues that within the one true and living God exists the Father, the Son and the Holy Spirit (Matthew 28:19-20).

Thus, I believe that Jesus Christ is the Son of God who died on the cross for our sins and rose again from the dead to give us eternal life if we would repent of our sins and place our faith in Him. I also believe that the Bible is God's inspired and infallible Word (2 Timothy 3:15-16).

I believe in the God of historic Christianity because this is the will of God for me in Christ Jesus Christ my Lord. I believe because God has given me faith to believe. I am because God has made me. I live and move and have my very being in God who says, "I Am that I AM" (Exodus 3:14).

Why do I believe in God? I am my beloveds and my beloved is mine! That is, God has demonstrated His own love for me in that while we were yet sinners, Christ died for us" (Romans 5:8).

I believe because God has opened my eyes to the truth of His Son Jesus Christ who is the savior of the world.

I believe in God because this is God's will for me. he has opened my eyes and heart to believe the good news of the Gospel of His Son our Lord Jesus Christ.

I do not believe in God because I am clever, because I am not.

I do not believe because I am an American (and I am).

I believe in God and His Son our Lord Jesus because this is the only way of salvation.

Jesus said, I am the way, the truth, and the life, no one comes to the Father except by Me" (John 14:6).

Jesus Christ died on the cross and rose again from the dead and appeared to over 500 people after He was crucified, buried and risen from the grave (1 Corinthians 15:1-7).

I believe in God because Jesus is risen from the dead and He is Lord!

Why is the Federal Government Spying on It's People?

Once upon a time there was a great Archangel. He was the greatest of all of God's angels until he started to break bad and was thrust out of heaven and from the majestic presence of the Lord of glory. In the process he took a third of the angels with him.

When Lucifer fell, he fell hard and when he spiraled from his lofty position, tumbling and stumbling to the earth, he thought of diverse ways to enslave men and women (Isaiah

14:12-15, Ezekiel 28:13-19, Luke 10:18, 2 Peter 2:4 and Revelation 12:9). Of all the dastardly plans the devil has concocted for humanity to do his diabolical bidding, one of the most perverse strategies was for him to convince a great portion of the world's populace to believe that they are servants to the State.

That is, they have bought into the fallacious thesis of known as *Statism (the view that the state should control social, economic and political activity in a given society)* that they exist to be subservient to professed elite class of individuals who run the governments of this world. A "State" is an organized community living under one government.

They have bought into the lie that we exist to serve the State and that everything we own create and aspire to do and be is a possession of the State. To quote Morpheus's verbal discourse to Neo in the Wachowski's cinematic masterpiece known as *The Matrix, you are a slave* if you believe that you exist to serve the self-appointed "elite" few.

You must realize that there are authoritarian political forces at work right now in the United States that actually believe that it is in your best interest that they control every aspect of your life. They want to subjugate you through social control. The elite few want to control your speech, thought, movements, money and essentially every aspect of your life. Right now, the government has the ability via drones to spy on your every move. The American government also has deemed it necessary to tap into your cell phone calls, bank account and essentially every other area of your life. We are being spied on, herded like chattel and assaulted by the very government we voted in to "protect" and serve us.

Case in point, most of us have bought into the absolute lie that to insure our safety we must be groped, probed and physically assaulted by the TSA every time we want to fly via commercial airlines. This is another form of social control. There is no evidence that the TSA's efforts are doing anything but shaming us silly at the airport each and every time we travel.

As a Libertarian, who believes in the maximization of human autonomy and freedom from the State's control, I greatly disdain and protest this government intrusion into our personal lives and will fight against it to my last dying breath. I would rather die on my feet than live on my knees as a slave and pawn to an elite ruling class who think they know what is best for me rather than I myself.

Like many lovers of freedom, I want to live free or die without drones spying on me and the TSA groping me every freaking time I travel by plane. I am calling for a Libertarian revolution against the encroachment of the moribund American government upon our civil liberties. I am calling for all those who want to live free of government control to join me against big brother. If you are bemused by this blog and think I am joking, just do a little research and see how much the government knows about you...

On Ayn Rand and Libertarianism

I have a confession to make. I love a woman. I know that may seem very unusual for many of you to read. I think I have built a reputation as some sort of indefatigable asexual Libertarian activist. However, contrary to some vicious rumors making the rounds in certain inhospitable circles, I do have a discernible sexuality.

Today I am making a bold profession of love for a woman. Forget the non – existent scandal laden rumors and get the scoop right here folks, I am in love with the greatest woman that has ever lived in my humble estimation.

Her name is Ayn Rand. You may have heard of her. You know the brilliant and bold Russian writer and philosopher who lived from 1905 to 1982. Ayn was a powerful woman and great testimony to what a woman can do to change society.

Ayn, as many of us know, was the founder of the self-determinist and Libertarian philosophy known as "Objectivism," that postulates the proper moral purpose of one's life is the pursuit of one's own happiness (rational self-interest), that the only social system consistent with this morality is one that displays full respect for individual rights embodied in laissez-faire capitalism.

I absolutely and passionately love Ayn Rand for writing incredibly enlightening books such as "The Fountainhead" and "Atlas Shrugged" and for teaching generations of people to live rewarding lives independent of external social controls and dependency on the State.

Ayn's whole philosophical project was a rejection of liberalism and statism that argue that human beings should live servile and dependent lives upon the State. She rejected the notion that an elite few individuals in the halls and shelter of government know what is best for our lives.

Millions of people around the world have been touched by Ayn's fierce pronouncement that we should live self-determined live for our own interests and personal happiness. I am one of these admirers.

However, much of her personal philosophy was hostile to Christianity and she rejected altruism (that we should live with selflessness, self-sacrifice and concern for others). As an atheist, she repudiated Christ's teachings and the Jesus Christ's death on the cross had any positive significance for humanity.

As a Libertarian I love Ayn Rand for teaching me that I must live my life with autonomy and fierce independence from the tyranny of the State.

However, as a devout Christian who believes that Jesus Christ is the Son of God who died on the cross for our sins and rose again from the dead to give humanity eternal life if we would turn from our sins and place our faith in Christ, I reject outright and in total Ayn Rand's atheism and hostility to Christianity.

I also reject Ayn Rand's views on altruism and believe that we should try to help others in need. Where I agree with her is that I do not believe human beings exist to further the State and that government should be limited and kept in check in order that it does not become abusive and tyrannical over its citizens which is often the case.

I also very much agree with her views on free market capitalism and that we should work hard to achieve our own dreams.

As a Christian, I reject much of Ayn Rand's Objectivist project despite its good elements. I believe there are things taught about self-determinism that can be appropriated into the Christian Worldview however. If Ayn Rand was still alive, and somehow I was able to become her friend, I would try to love her as Christ did and show her that the Bible is God's inerrant and inspired Word and that life is futile without God. I would also try to write to her and show her that Jesus Christ is the only avenue to salvation.

Jesus said, "I am the way, the truth, and the life, no one comes to the Father except by Me" (John 14:6).

"For neither is there salvation in any other, for there is no other name under heaven (except Jesus) by which people can be saved" (Acts 4:12).

I love Ayn Rand and pray that she came to a saving knowledge of Jesus before she died.

"But these have been written that you might believe that Jesus is the Christ, the Son of God and that by believing, you might have life in His name" (John 20:32).

Introducing Christian Libertarianism

I hate philosophy.

By "philosophy" I mean the study of worldly wisdom or the vain attempt of human beings to understand the essence and meaning of human existence outside of God. Now, I know what you might be thinking. Why would I introduce a new way of looking at life if I hate philosophical discussion? On the contrary,

I do not hate philosophical discussion *per se.* I simply detest and do not have any time for any worldview of train of thought that does not seriously consider the thoughts and teachings of the greatest person that has ever lived, namely Jesus Christ.

Above everything, I want to be a Biblical Christian who predicates my belief system on the explicit teachings of God's inerrant and inspired Word (2 Timothy 3:15-16). I personally outright reject any philosophical system or ideological proposition that does not place the Lord Jesus Christ as the center of the discussion. For all the treasures of wisdom and knowledge are hid in Jesus Christ (Colossians 2:3-8).

From the onset, I want to be made perfectly clear. I am a Christian who believes in the absolute supremacy of Jesus Christ over all things. I believe Jesus Christ died on the cross for our sins and rose again from the dead to give us eternal life if we repent of our sins and place our faith in Him. I believe this based on the perfect authority of God's Word.

In the political realm I want to introduce a bold concept I call "Christian Libertarianism," which is the belief that people should be free to serve God in the liberty of their conscience without external coercion and compulsion. I personally believe that the best government is the least amount of government and the citizens of the State should be free to serve God without social controls. Thus, the Christian Libertarian believes in all the essential doctrinal truths of the historic Christian faith such as the doctrine of the Trinity, the Deity and Virgin Birth, justification by grace through faith in Jesus Christ alone and the authority, inspiration and inerrancy of the Bible alone.

The Christian Libertarian also believes that human beings should be free in society to make decisions that flow from their own individual consciences and not be coerced to do something that violates ones conscience and power of choice.

I believe that we must strive to be free from all external forms of control. We must be free and autonomous from the intrusive power of the State as well. I personally believe that the best government is the least amount of government and that we must strive to free ourselves from the idolatry of State worship and dependence. That is, we must free ourselves from a tendency to look to one's government to meet his or her basic needs.

Christian Libertarianism is a worldview that says that we must be free from the idolatry of the State in order to be free to serve God without external controls.

Christian Libertarianism (Latin: liber, "free") is a political and theological worldview that upholds liberty under the

Lordship of Jesus Christ as its principal objective.
Christian Libertarians seek to obey God as the Bible mandates and to maximize autonomy and freedom of choice, emphasizing political freedom, voluntary association and the primacy of individual judgment.

Christian Libertarianism is simply a Christian view of politics and interaction in society that puts forth the premise that men and women should be able to live under the Lordship of Christ in a manner that maximizes human autonomy and freedom. Christian Libertarians seek to obey God and live as free as possible from external controls and authoritarian coercion.

My journey towards more of a Libertarian perspective has a lot to do with that I have seen and experienced in Southern Baptist and Evangelical fundamentalist circles. While I am very much a Christian, I am entirely burned out with churches and schools that try to micro-manage every aspect of our lives. I believe in personal liberty and the right for each of us to live as our consciences dictates.

Too often, I have seen unhealthy spirituality and authoritarianism cloaked in pietistic religiosity that sounds "biblical" but, is in the end just as bad as any other form of soul-quenching, individualism destroying and personal freedom robbing authoritarianism seen in the secular realm.

I find it interesting that many conservatives spend their lives fighting against the tyranny of the politically correct left and it's forced conformity to certain progressive dogmas, yet unwittingly place themselves under another form of authoritarian social control.

Be wary of any church, religious leader or religious school, college, university or seminary that tries to micromanage, manipulate or conform you to ad hoc and artificially generated standards and expectations that are not explicitly delineated in God's inerrant and infallible Word.

Much of American Evangelicalism and Fundamentalist Christianity in this country is ruled and lorded over by toxic, unhealthy and abusive control-freaks that are looking for filial acolytes and unquestioned fidelity to their cult of personalities. Often these religious leaders couch their personal enrichment in religious language and do not allow any questioning of their personal fiefdoms.

After many decades in American Evangelical, Southern Baptist and Fundamentalist Christian circles, where I have seen myriads of instances of abuse and lives ruined, I am daring to speak out against an insidious form of authoritarianism that is sadly all too common in America.

I want to be clear; I am a Christian and believe in the authority of Scripture. I believe in the doctrine of the Trinity, the Deity of Christ, justification by faith in Christ alone and every other essential and fundamental doctrine of historic Christianity.

I also want to be clear that I believe in biblical and healthy authority in the local Church and believe that pastors, elders and deacons have the right to exercise their authority and church discipline in their respective Christian assemblies.

I also believe that each Christian that makes up a given Christian church has the God-given and Biblical right to question authority and ask questions about how things are operating in their churches. Yet, all too often, believers in respective Evangelical churches are told they can never question anything or anyone in their churches and must submit to the rule of their elders without question or exception.

I am also not an "antinomian" or a person who lives their life without the moral law found in God's Word. On the contrary, I believe we all must submit to the authority of Christ as found in the Bible and attempt to live godly and exemplary lives by the power of the Holy Spirit.

I am simply writing this to say that many conservative Christians in this country have and are unwittingly submitting themselves to an authoritarian pattern of social control that is just as insidious and damaging as any form of tyranny they perceive is occurring on the left of the political and cultural divide.

I am personally advocating a form of "Christian Libertarianism," a conservative expression of political philosophy that allows people to serve God under the Lordship of Christ with personal liberty and individual conscience.

After years of attending some of American Evangelicalism's most prominent schools and churches, I know all too well the culture I come from. I know all too well that many will call me a heretic and an "antinomian," which is simply not true. I believe in every word of the Bible and the Westminster Confession of Faith and want to obey God.

Why I am a Libertarian Republican

I have a confession to make. I am a Libertarian. To those who have recently met me that is not much of a surprise because that is all that I seem to talk about. I spend most of my waking hours thinking about how I can further the cause of Libertarianism, the political philosophy that best exemplifies my own personal worldview.

Libertarianism (Latin: liber, "free") is a political philosophy that upholds liberty and human autonomy as its principal objectives. Libertarians seek to maximize autonomy and freedom of choice, emphasizing political freedom, voluntary association and the primacy of individual judgment.

I can no longer follow the Republican Party status quo and will only support Republican and Libertarian candidates that are fiercely against government interference in our personal and economic lives. I believe that the best government is the least amount of government period.

Recent incidents of violent crime in the United States have caused me to speak out against the mayhem and murderous anarchy that has engulfed out city streets. The recent murders of young people in San Francisco, Chicago and Washington D.C. demonstrate that the politicians in Washington D.C. need to do better at ending crime that runs rampant on our city streets.

In Defense of Capitalism

Capitalism, an economic and political system in which a country's trade and industry are controlled by private owners for profit, rather than by the state, is under siege in America. One only needs to walk on the average college and university campus in America and find out that Capitalism is not very popular in academic settings these days.

During this time period of western civilization, the United States of America faces a very uncertain future due to catastrophic and systemic fiscal problems. At the time of this writing, America's national debt has mushroomed to over seventeen trillion dollars and economists estimate that forty-three cents of every dollar earned in this country is borrowed, which is about four times the rate of deficit spending America incurred in 1980.

Due to this massive national debt and deficit spending, many people around the country are arguing that the current financial model operating in the United States is unsustainable and some other are even arguing that free market capitalism should not be the foundational economic system of this nation.

In the face of these persistent calls of overhauling America's economic system, this current author would like to argue that free market capitalism is the economic model most compatible with the economic principles delineated by the authors of sacred Scripture and, that free market capitalism should be maintained as the fiscal model for America's economy.

The subject of economics has taken center stage in recent political discussions in the United States and it is of paramount importance that American Evangelicals be knowledgeable of the fiscal problems that currently plague this country in order to be effective ambassadors of life to the culture in which God has called Christians to minister.

The recent "Occupy Wall Street Movement" and cultural ascendancy and trenchant leftist policy implementation of President Barack Obama has made the subject of economics pertinent to every concerned American. President Obama, by his own admission is a progressive and left leaning politician who has decried the alleged economic injustices fiscal abuses of recent Republican administrations and the free market system and has attempted to level the playing field between rich and poor in American society through economic policy change and a more activist role of the federal government.

While many people in America claim to be "socialist" hardly anyone adopts this as their overall economic system. Socialism is a political and economic theory of social organization that advocates that the means of production, distribution, and exchange should be owned or regulated by the community as a whole.

I find it interesting that while many college town liberals and academics decry capitalism and argue for a socialist and even communist economic system, the book stores of our colleges and universities gouge us students with marked up prices to earn a profit! Most self-professed socialists and communists I have encountered are not consistent with their beliefs and utilize the capitalist model in almost all their economic activities.

Hillary Rides the Beast

"And I stood upon the sand of the sea, and saw a beast rise up out of the sea" (Revelation 13:1).

For over two millennia Biblical scholars and other astute interpreters of inspired Christian Scripture have given conjecture over what the meaning of "the beast" is in the ancient apocalyptic book of Revelation.

In this last book of the New Testament, the Apostle John, while exiled on the island of Patmos, saw the beast "rise up out of the sea, having seven heads and ten horns, and upon his horns ten crowns, and upon his heads the name of blasphemy." (Revelation 13:1) The beast was like a leopard, with feet like the feet of a bear, and had a mouth like a lion.

Some have argued that "the beast" is a person, other say it is a corporation or body of people. While Biblical scholars are not in exact agreement over the identity of "the beast," one thing is for sure, "the beast" is something massive and sinister…

Here is that wild Libertarian on the move again, this time I am at my father's cattle ranch down home in Texas. Today I discuss Hillary Clinton's lack of honesty about the Benghazi crisis and clear inaccuracies about not being subpoenaed when she in fact was.

In Washington Hillary Clinton drew stinging Republican criticism Wednesday after falsely claiming she had never been subpoenaed for emails from her time as secretary of state.

When CNN's Brianna Keilar asked Clinton in an exclusive interview on Tuesday about the decision to delete 33,000 emails while under investigation by a House panel, Clinton said other secretaries of state had done the "same thing."

In this video on the family cattle ranch in Crawford, I also discuss how "Hillary Rides the Beast." That, is, Ms. Clinton has a beast of burden like this horse, trying to explain her personal enrichment from corporate speaking engagements that have earned her and her husband, the former President Bill Clinton millions of dollars

The Case Against Bernie Sanders

I like comic books and was a voracious collector of all things Marvel growing up until one day upon returning from Junior High, my sainted mother, in a Dr. Spock enlightened moment, threw my entire collection of Marvel Comics away. I was stunned to say the least. "Stunned" is actually not the best word to describe my deep and abiding angst I felt when mother went rogue on me and tossed my stash.

Now, you have to understand the great lengths and considerable efforts I went through to procure these illustrated treasures featuring Spidey, Hulk, Capitan America and his prodigious compadres. I also liked some DC comic book heroes but not so much since it those days one was either a Marvel Comic fan or a DC Comic enthusiast. Normally one did not cross over to the dark side and buy a comic from the rival brand.

However, one DC title that I absolutely adored was the "Watchmen." I found the alternative reality and parallel universe in the story line fascinating. A parallel universe is a hypothetical self-contained separate reality co-existing with one's own. In the Watchman's parallel universe Richard Nixon is President in 1980's and superheroes in spandex jumpsuits such as Dr. Manhattan are needed to save the word.

Recently I have felt that I was in some sort of alternative universe when I saw that the far left and socialist Senator Bernie Sanders was surging in the polls in his bid to win the Democratic nomination for President.

Sanders is an independent Senator who caucuses with the Democrats and has previously ran as candidate for various offices under the banner of the leftist Liberty Union and Vermont Progressive parties.

Sanders is a true believer in the progressive agenda and his voting record in the House of Representatives and Senate clearly bears this out. Sanders is so Liberal he made the progressives Barrack Obama, Paul Wellstone and Howard Dean seem like hopeless moderates.

Sanders' voting record clearly shows that there is not a piece of progressive legislation and entitlement appropriations bill he does not want and believes the federal government should flip the bill for it all

Sanders has spent his entire adult life running for one office or another and his progressive voting record is clear for all to see.

In the coming days as both the Republican and Democratic primaries start heating up, I will be commenting on both Bernie Sanders and Hillary Clinton and will do everything in my power to campaign against them.

As a Pro-life Republican with Libertarian sympathies, I believe Bernie Sanders, if elected, will most certainly bankrupt this country with all his entitlement programs. Like President Obama, he does not seem to be able to grasp that all these social programs he campaigns for cost money, lots of money that we simply do not have. Right now America is spiraling down into a black hole of debt with a 17 trillion dollar and rising national deficit and Sanders is either oblivious or incapable of realizing that America cannot continue to spend money that it does not have.

I simply refuse to be a part of the cradle to the grave entitlements approach that Sanders advocates since it makes one entirely dependent upon the government for one's basic needs. I personally believe that Bernie Sander's big and expansive model of government stifles human autonomy and impendence and makes one a servant of the socialist state. Progressives like Bernie Sanders always have big plans for spending our hard earned money on their entitlement programs and special interest legislation, but they never get around to telling us how we can spend it or lower the national debt.

I for one want to live as a free man with the wind to my back and my future ahead of me as the master of my own destiny and servant of none. As a proponent of small and radically down-sized government, I simply believe Bernie Sanders vision of single payer health insurance and economic equality for all translates into economic dependence on the federal government.

Bernie Sanders has made his career as an advocate for the disadvantaged and those who cannot fend for themselves. I find ironic that in the case of the unborn, the ultimate people group that need our care, he turns his back on. As a person who believes that life begins at conception, I also cannot in good conscience vote for one like Bernie Sanders who does not advocate for the life of the unborn.

At stake here is a fundamentally different vision for America and the quality of life. On one hand we can adopt the big government model of Bernie Sanders who believes the federal government should be involved in every area of our lives or a Libertarian vision for America that frees us to be dependent upon no one except ourselves and God.

Please look at the voting record of Bernie Sanders I have provided, it will show exactly how much of a socialist he really is. This alternative reality is something America can do without.

On the Stupid Ariana Grande Scandal

If you have not heard, there is a scandal of epic scandal transpiring in America and it is just beginning. In fact, many pundits and astute observers of American culture are openly questioning if we can survive as a collective society.

The whole ordeal broke and went viral when TMZ released a video of the unquestionably talented 22 year old pop princess known for her classic songs, "Bang Bang," "Problem," and "Love Me Harder," went into a Southern California doughnut shop and licked some unsuspecting doughnuts. Furthermore, Ms. Grande is heard on the new video saying, "I hate America."

Gasp! I know I was mortally wounded and all my dreams were crushed when I heard the video myself. The fact that a 22 year old girl with such a massive fan base could openly lick some doughnuts meant for public consumption and then publicly shatter the lives of hundreds of millions of people by disrespecting God and country like that is beyond human comprehension.

According to Associated News, Ms. Grande herself announced Wednesday that she would not perform at the MLB All-Star Concert on Saturday, but said it had nothing to do with a leaked video that led her to make a public apology.

"As for why I cannot be at the MLB show, I have had emergency oral surgery and due to recovery I cannot attend the show," she said. "That being said let me once again apologize if I have offended anyone with my poor choice of words."

Police and Federal Prosecutors said Wednesday they were investigating video that appears to show Ms. Grande licking doughnuts at this shop in Southern California. Earlier, Grande apologized for saying"I hate America" in the same video.

AP says that Police in Lake Elsinore, where the doughnut shop is located, said they and Riverside County public health officials were investigating the leaked video, which appeared to show the 22-year-old singer and a man with her "maliciously lick" the doughnuts.

According to AP, Mayra Solis, 22, a cashier on duty at Wolfe Donuts when Grande went into the store, said the singer didn't purchase any of the doughnuts she licked. "She was really rude," Solis told The Associated Press.

Earlier Wednesday, Grande said in a statement to the AP that she's a proud American.

"I am EXTREMELY proud to be an American and I've always made it clear that I love my country. What I said in a private moment with my friend, who was buying the doughnuts, was taken out of context and I am sorry for not using more discretion with my choice of words," the statement read.

Can America survive? Stay tuned. What is definitely known is that this is a crisis of epic proportions that all of us should focus all of our attention around and sit in stunned silence until it is resolved.

This morning, while the news of Ariana Grande's doughnut licking scandal was rocking a stunned nation, I took to the mean streets here in Princeton, New Jersey to find out the pulse of the people on this issue. This video shows one man's concern for America as we know it.

(This spoofed story was adapted from Fox News' Article; "Ariana Grande out of ASG concert amid doughnut licking scandal," July 8, 2015).

"Where the Spirt of the Lord is there is liberty" (2 Corinthians 3:17).

Can a person be a Libertarian and a Christian at the same time? This may sound like an unusual question to some people and depending on your ideological reference point; you might attempt to answer the question in various ways. There is a popular belief held by many well-meaning people that in order to be a dedicated Christian you must at once be apolitical or a socialist in your views on the relationship between human beings, economics and the government. In many academic and religious settings the very notion that one could be a devout and dedicated Christian and believe in self-determinism and human autonomy is heterodox and contrary to collectivist and statist sentiments.

Well, we here at Rogue Reformation, based on the authority of the Bible alone, believe in the doctrines of the historic Christian faith and maintain that it is possible to a Christian and a Libertarian at the same time and believe there is radical misinformation being disseminated out there about what Libertarianism is. In all actuality a Christian Libertarian is one who believes that Jesus Christ alone if Lord of all and not the State.

The Christian Libertarian believes and promotes a view of radical autonomy and independence from government intrusion and interference in our personal, economic and religious lives. We believe that God alone is king and not the State and strive to be free to serve God as we feel called by the Almighty. We believe in personal liberty to serve God and our fellow human beings as our personal convictions and consciences dictate. We have no king but Jesus.

I proud to present to you this collection of essays in defense of liberty and Rand Paul.

Kind Regards,

Lee Enochs
Princeton, NJ

www.ingramcontent.com/pod-product-compliance
Lightning Source LLC
Chambersburg PA
CBHW020521290526
45786CB00002B/699